LETTERS
TO THE
HOLY ONE

LUCE

authorHOUSE®

AuthorHouse™
1663 Liberty Drive
Bloomington, IN 47403
www.authorhouse.com
Phone: 1 (800) 839-8640

Published by AuthorHouse 11/18/2019

ISBN: 978-1-7283-3577-3 (sc)
ISBN: 978-1-7283-3575-9 (hc)
ISBN: 978-1-7283-3576-6 (e)

Prayer Book Page 1

Sat, 31 Mar 2012 18:40:19

Eternal God, Jesus, Love

Embrace in your holy

Healing mercy

My reaching - to be

One with you

Share, in spirit

Your love – Suffering

On the cross

Leave this heart wounded beyond repair

Love – Purifying

Jesus, fill empty and longing

Desires – your wounds

See in eyes hidden

Humble spirit giving thanks

Long hours – Agony

Your dying on the cross – Salvation

Prayer Book Page 2

Tue, 03 Apr 2012 21:05:41

Eternal God, Jesus, Love

In you my spirit lives

Beyond all merit

Kissed in Resurrection

Fragrance

Accept prayers purified

In your wounds

Living in your Rising

Forgiveness – lift me up

To heaven's rim

Angels singing

In your light

Condemn the darkness

Lest I fail to see

Your glory

Break the ties

That bind me

Concealing holy ways

Come now my love

Be the rest of my days

If you do not love me

My God I cannot love

But remain in deadness

As a stone

Prayer Book Page 3

Fri, 06 Apr 2012 18:23:23

Eternal God, Jesus, Love

The joy of You

Lives in every heart

Yearning....

All creation knows

The joy of You

Free – Devine Love....

Jesus, joy of joys

Living Bread of Life....

Jesus, giving the greatest joy

In Resurrection

All mankind

Thrives in You – Eternal Life....

Jesus, the joy of your wounds

Your sorrow, suffering

Thirst

Drawing all to share the joy of You....

Lord Jesus

For all who believe

Your Kingdom waits....

Prayer Book Page 4

Tue, 10 Apr 2012 21:06:09

Eternal God, Jesus, Love

How long my love

Have I reached for you

How long has my heart

Carried the burden of loneliness

You are not there…

If this is to be

My suffering

Impress it

For the joy of you

Grace allow

Let me hold your hand….

Thirsting in my heart

Anguish for you my love

My spirit weeps

Your consuming embrace….

There is no joy

Beyond you, Jesus

There is no comfort

Beyond your cross

There is no peace, Jesus

Like unto the peace you give….

Prayer Book Page 5

Thu, 12 Apr 2012 19:08:33

Eternal God, Jesus, Love

Fill the fields of my heart

Fragrant blossoms

Holy angels singing

Sweetness of your love….

See the Lady

All in white

Like the sun

Brilliant light

Calling out as it can only be

Love and hope – tenderly

In the garden of life

Where angels play

Lanterns burning

Guide the way ….

Spirit firm and true

In fragrance rejoice

Join hands in delight

She waits there

The Lady – all in white…

Prayer Book Page 6

Sun, 15 Apr 2012 20:23:27

Eternal God, Jesus, Love

Heart blending

Spirit praying – pleading

Shared suffering

Eternal life….

No suffering contains meaning – purpose

If You are not within

You alone – Jesus

Elevate suffering

Divinity

Living in the same veins

Where sorrow travels….

The weight of the cross

Not yours alone

One thorn or every thorn

One wound or every wound

One nail or every nail

One drop of blood or every drop

One lash or every lash

End bondage

In the freedom of your love

Give sanctuary

To the forgiven heart

Reaching for You....

Prayer Book Page 7

Sat, 21 Apr 2012 18:58:50

Eternal God, Jesus, Love

Mother weeps - her children

Through dark nights

Souls cold – alarmed

There is loss – serious to tell

Many gathering – leaving….

What voice – lamenting calls

Did they follow – turning away

His cross always there – brilliant

Promise – hope – redemption

Lights breathing through the heavens….

Why did they turn

Away from the only one

Giving magnificent love

Eternal life – salvation

Rising is forever His….

Through each lifetime

She waits to welcome

And embrace

Those arriving with unspent desire

For his light

As darkness

Crushes

Frozen hearts….

Prayer Book Page 8

Tue, 24 Apr 2012 21:04:26

Eternal God, Jesus, Love

Silent earth

So few praying

Pain – suffering – rampant

Raging storm

Where is kindness

Caring hearts – in prayer

Pouring out – healing love

End the storm – pain – sorrow….

No strangers here

Crying for prayers of love

Embrace another – take suffering

Into your spirit….

Be comfort – in all afflictions

Gather hurt and tears

Hold in divine embrace

Healing love – your gift unseen….

Give voice to earth

It is true

Life and peace

Depend on you….

Prayer Book Page 9

Tue, 24 Apr 2012 21:14:46

Eternal God, Jesus, Love

A special prayer

For someone unknown

It matters not – chance never met

Prayer enters the heart of God

Faith reveals

Prayers see God

When hearts live in every word….

Holy God – Jesus

Open your sacred heart

Let this prayer enter

Send abundant grace

Your divine – holy – eternally

Healing love – mercy – compassion

Give freedom from all disease – affliction

Spiritual – physical – mental – emotional….

Holy God – Jesus

Let the power of your love

Heal all

Who reach for you

In this prayer…

Prayer Book Page 10

Sun, 29 Apr 2012 15:49:55

Eternal God, Jesus, Love

A great light rising

Sublime joy impressing

Within all who seek….

Light – giving life

Warming – comforting – compelling

Live in me – that I may not live

Be in me – that I not be

Your breath – breath of my soul

Your voice – my voice

Your words – from my lips

There is no joy - but you Jesus….

Create anew – what has faded

Make again bright and beautiful

In your eyes – soul seeking

Desires only you Jesus

Empty me into supreme happiness

Your sweet love

Only then will I be free

Consumed forever – your divinity…

Prayer Book Page 11

Sun, 29 Apr 2012 15:55:54

Eternal God, Jesus, Love

Before the hour ends

Please your hand

Lift me up

Defeat the darkness….

Purpose of my love

Delay the nearing dawn

Send angels to sing

Let peace be sanctuary…

The only truth – love

Holding every heart

Gold rays swirl within

Risen glory

Live again

Before the hour ends….

Out beyond the heavens

Where whispers speak

If I disappear

Do not mourn

In God

A new and beautiful star is born…

Prayer Book Page 12

Tue, 01 May 2012 19:21:45

Eternal God, Jesus, Love

Word – crucified

Calling – Father

Forgive them

Angry hands – deny

Suffering – love…

Here another in pain

Reaching – receiving – offerings

Radiating from the Cross

Holding – pierced heart

Word crucified….

Impossible to understand

Depth of hate

Soaking the ground

With His blood

Answering the nails

Forgiving love….

In the end – gasping

Commending spirit

Father – waiting

Earth breaking

Heaven – silent

Word – ascended…

Prayer Book Page 13

Sun, 06 May 2012 10:56:14

Eternal God, Jesus, Love

The grace of You

Reveals

Each time my fears rise

Your heart opens

Offering a place

For my prayers to live

My spirit rest

Such splendid love....

Only in Your grace – my love

My prayers speak Your name

How wonderful – You come to me

Giving me the joy of You

Gentle peace....

Your caring love – guides me

As I walk in Your light

The kingdom waits to welcome

Live in the joy of You....

My prayers reach for You

My only desire

Life anew

In the grace of You

Forever – unchanging....

Prayer Book Page 14

Sun, 13 May 2012 21:39:24

Eternal God, Jesus, Love

You gave this prayer

Sweetness of your love

Softening pain – freeing spirit

You embrace each heart

Rejoicing – healing….

Your words rise softly

Filling each moment – calming whispers

In the midst of suffering – peace

Your heart touches…

Giving God – loving – caring God

Holding all in your prayer

Let those who speak your words

Know you call them from the cross

To leave their suffering

In your blood

The prayer you have given

Breath – eternal life….

With his prayer in your heart

Jesus lives in you

With his words on your lips

You live in Jesus….

Prayer Book Page 15

Fri, 18 May 2012 19:45:18

Eternal God, Jesus, Love

The lady in white returned

First glance – upset

Her smile – peace overwhelming…

Clarification – understanding

With spirit in suspension

Reaching ended – in her purity…

Hold onto this

My son lives in the very heart

Of your pain and suffering

Were it not true

You would perish quickly….

Every moment you suffer

Hold my son – He alone is your need

Speak his name often – His love

Carries you through so many difficulties

Beyond your understanding…

Give Him your suffering – not for self

For another – somewhere suffering alone

Let your tears fill His pierced heart

Returning in His love – peace – comfort

Through my Son – your offering

Healing for someone unknown to you

Even to the entering of the kingdom….

Prayer Book Page 16

Fri, 22 Jun 2012 19:17:06

Eternal God, Jesus, Love

This day – great joy

Celebration – Now

Your invitation has arrived

Happiness beyond

The meagerness of my being

Banquet to spend my life

In total union – with You….

Joy of joys – true – living joy

Radiating – embracing

Such splendor – cannot remain locked

In one heart – bursting….

Jesus, you are the sweetest love

Lifting beyond belief

Holding my spirit….

Let my joy consume forever

You are freedom

Jesus, there is no joy

More joyful than you

In your arms - seeking is ended…

Prayer Book Page 17

Thu, 05 Jul 2012 18:59:08

Eternal God, Jesus, Love

Yes, I heard you calling

Just above a whisper

Not so sure

You were there

I wondered – Me - Calling me

How is it possible

Calling me…

Noise in and around you

Is condemned

Were I to shout

For your attention

Earth would crumble

You   no longer…

My voice reaches you

When your heart is open

Waiting – prayer in place

Speaking my name

With love and longing

As my own…

My voice embraces you

In a whisper

Come - be with me

Fear not the thunder

Live in my grace – in the whisper

Prayer Book Page 18

Thu, 05 Jul 2012 19:07:07

Eternal God, Jesus, Love

Yes, I was there

Alone

In the darkness and the silence

At the very edge of hell

Existing as emptiness

Beyond the reach

Of goodness…

Yes, you intervened

Retrieving me

No surrender

To the second way of death

Back into light

From your hand

I lived again…

Only then

Could I feel

My trembling

Knowing fear

Until you erased it all

In the light of you

I lived again….

Prayer Book Page 19

Sun, 22 Jul 2012 17:01:57

Eternal God, Jesus, Love

Yes, my Love

Your angel declared the gift

In my time of suffering

Wrapped in the sweetest love

From the depths of your divinity

How beautiful – hope…

Through all of my suffering

Never once lessening

My clinging to you

Compressed in my heart

Your gift

There is no hope as pure as you…

Peace comes to devour

Raging pain

Hope fills my heart

Refreshing spring

Flooding me

Your healing love…

The joy of hope

Your heart

Holding eternally

My own – hope so glorious…

Prayer Book Page 20

Sun, 29 Jul 2012 13:53:05

Eternal God, Jesus, Love

Again

Unseen

You are here – the river flows

Truth – of life remains – hidden

Unable to keep restrained

Reaching for the unseen begins

Why do you come so quietly?

Confounding me

While my spirit weeps

Thrashing in cold emptiness

Remembering your embrace

So long ago

Sweetest love

Holding

My spirit succumbs

Now – sweetest love – thirst extreme

No thought for ending

Rapture - eternal moment

Sweetest love

Mine again

Ever lasting

Caressed

My eyes holding – without seeing

My spirit breathes

In your sweetest love

Prayer Book Page 21

Fri, 03 Aug 2012 19:02:26

Eternal God, Jesus, Love

Waiting for you

Quiet night covering

Darkness remaining undisturbed

With beads in hand

Silence continuing

Tears praying – Your love

Is there a saint – seeking

Softness called

No my love – no saint here

Maybe one of the worst

Who claims – no one loves you more

Your heart is open

Ask of me

Into my heart – sweet love

The gentleness of you

A place to hide – quiet purification

Go there – my light lives in the cross

Share with me

My pain – my suffering

In every wound my love

Take me down – free me from the wood

In your love

Your gentleness

Comfort me

Prayer Book Page 22

Mon, 13 Aug 2012 12:25:58

Eternal God, Jesus, Love

Time turning new

Sparkling bright – days known

In the embrace of your way

Distance no longer meaning

Time turning new

Sparkling bright

Filled with joy

Then – now – forever love

Listen – laughter

Joy consuming

Time turning new

Sparkling bright

Beyond dreams

Smile again

Time singing

In your embrace – my love

Time spent – lives again

So little attention given

Now so precious

Sparkling bright

Beyond the line

In your love – life is

Forever

New

Prayer Book Page 23

Mon, 20 Aug 2012 18:49:51

Eternal God, Jesus, Love

Voice of your heart

Lifted me – into the warmth

Of your love

Reaching for understanding

Pain and suffering – endured.

Spiritual shades fade

Into groans– graces lost

Conclusions – lies

Pain and suffering

Bury the heart – empty faith

Prayers fade from lips

Frozen in the memories of good ways

My love – you are the purest love

Impossible for you to inflict

Pain and suffering

No contradictions

Your heart gives only love

Reveal to the broken

From whence

These come – pain and suffering

Embrace – granting fully

Your glorious mercy – triumphant

Healing love

Prayer Book Page 24

Tue, 04 Sep 2012 19:28:00

Eternal God, Jesus, Love

Last night, my love – awake long into the night

Praying for help in the darkness

Some things are difficult to understand.

Thousands of times in my years

Your name has come to me

Now my heart weeps – as your name

Caresses my lips -warming my spirit

Each one I placed in your

Loving heart – for healing

Some things are difficult to understand

With eyes closed – searching the distance

Hoping for a light

To guide my prayers – ending

Pain and suffering

Some things are just too difficult to understand

When will your kingdom come

End the mystery – of it's being

Until then it will remain

Difficult to understand

This suffering – this pain.

Prayer Book Page 25

Fri, 07 Sep 2012 19:25:22

Eternal God, Jesus, Love

Watching as your hand

Opened the heavens

Sending forth a great burst of light

Upon the earth – consuming darkness

Evil could be seen fleeing

Fear filled – in the pending doom

Fire from the lake in pursuit

No cries could be heard

No tears seen

Time for the ending

Evil in agony – dying

Your voice thundered through the light

Evil has hurt my children

I will bring them back new

They will live in me – happy – rejoicing

You wicked will be no more

That which you serve will perish with you

My creation will never again

Know evil

My seventh day

My day of rest

Is ending

Prayer Book Page 26

Mon, 24 Sep 2012 19:08:41

Eternal God, Jesus, Love

Your calling pierced the night

Bringing frantic spiritual displays

In the depths of my being

To the angels I cried for help

Ease the agony of his thirst

They turned – saying

Search your heart

He seeks what is there

In giving you find peace

He alone calms your spirit

Empty your heart into his

He waits for your gift

What do they see – hidden to me

How can I end – the pain of his thirst

In the silence – discovery

His calling is for love – my love

His thirst – the way of grace

Calling me – to his embrace

Prayer Book Page 27

Thu, 04 Oct 2012 19:42:22

Eternal God, Jesus, Love

Lifted in spirit – waiting

High above a great distance

Secure in brilliant light

So magnificent – glorious beauty

Burning into my soul

Love flared – bursting into furious flames

My spirit trembled

Your sympathy for the sick

Draws me close to you

Remember – their healing is in my hands

Be not troubled for this

They are not forgotten – or abandoned

Keep in mind – your turn will come

Time will be slow – doubts will rise

Loneliness – weeping – calls for prayers

Give each moment to me

We will be held together – in my light

Pray intensely now – for hours given

Free of pain and suffering

Do not waste time – asking why

I alone have allowed all that has ever been

All that is now I allow

All that will ever be

Will come through me

Even your existence

From the beginning to the end

Prayer Book Page 28

Thu, 18 Oct 2012 22:28:26

Eternal God, Jesus, Love

They were singing

So sweetly in the garden – earth

Wanting all to turn

Seek endlessly – the Great One

His love is Life

Children playing – laughter rising

Fragrance fills the garden – earth

Blossoms – new and fresh

Sing to the angels – joining sweetness

Children of the garden – earth

Gather with the angels

The Lady in white has returned

Embracing them in profound peace

Tears of joy nourish

A tender heavenly touch

Angels crying - unable to sing

Knowing the children of earth

Long for the Lady in white

To stay with them

Until the end of time

She will return and carry them

To a new home

The beautiful of garden of heaven.

Prayer Book Page 29

Thu, 18 Oct 2012 22:29:39

Eternal God, Jesus, Love

My love why does that distance exist

Holding me in separation

From the joy of you

Sometimes you are very close

Still only a blind man stands in front of you

Maybe it is because

Your presence is so overpowering

And mysterious

Obscuring my eyes

What of my spirit

Enduring such pain

Lost in the darkness of our light

Without consolation

Left to wander in hopeful visions

My love soften the splendor

Of your presence

Gain for me some measure of you

Knowing these eyes will never see you as they are

Please my love

Hold me in the eternal

Grace of you

Prayer Book Page 30

Thu, 18 Oct 2012 22:31:37

Eternal God, Jesus, Love

Walking for such a long time

My love

Not much is clear

As to purpose and meaning

Should your hand slip away – for sure

My soul will be lost

Walking has a long way to go

I yearn for the peace

Only you can give

There is a place – along the way

A place where angels sing

Their prayers bring lights

Like the stars – their words sparkle

Stop me there – let me enjoy

Quiet and peace – embracing

Watching the last time

The ocean moved away

Time crystalized

And vanished

There is still a long way to walk

Before the final breath

Brings eternal calm

Prayer Book Page 31

Mon, 22 Oct 2012 19:20:41

Eternal God, Jesus, Love

My love – this heart has flown

Deep into the grace of your mercy

Forgiveness – blessings – overflowing

Pleading – no longer needed

Mighty one – gentleness supreme

No tears – truth is known

Prayers reach you

Lord of all – loving all

Consume the fullness

Of my spirit – dissolve my shadow into you

Leave nothing

Let me be no more

No reason to continue

In you all is claimed

Coming forth – in a new beginning

Magnificent spirit – eternal

Caress the longing soul

Comfort – one yearning to live free in you

Bless in total grace – your love

One deprived – concealed

From the light – living

Prayer Book Page 32

Fri, 26 Oct 2012 18:57:37

Eternal God, Jesus, Love

There was a man here

Just after the light of day faded

It was a very bad situation

My effort to help – restrained

Someone through a stone

Striking him

No time to rage – the bloodied one

Collapsed at my feet – unable to rise

His cross was just too heavy

Looking at him staggered me

Soaked in blood – whipping went on

Without mercy – screaming and yelling

Relentless for his death

Help was needed – he could not lift the cross

Looking into his eyes – his love

Touched me – filling my spirit with great sorrow

Unable to hold him – comfort him

In my desire – a lash crossed my face

Falling against him – a thorn pierced my hand

Throwing my arms around him

Helping to lift the cross

There she was – holding him

The lady in white

Weeping for her son

Prayer Book Page 33

Wed, 31 Oct 2012 16:12:42

Eternal God, Jesus, Love

Since finding you – life changed

Great joy comes in the smallest moments

There can never be a day – from this one

Lived without you my Lord Jesus

My happiness lives in the truth of you

Joyfully hours pass in peace

No longer do worries entangle

And grip my spirit

Days once engulfed in turmoil

Are now calm

Since finding you a wonderful peace lives within

You live in me – I am not

No lingering fears   since finding you

Afflictions so terribly heavy dissolve in your grace

Since finding you

Life will never end

Knowing forever

Precious gift the joy of you

In your magnificent love

Prayer Book Page 34

Sun, 04 Nov 2012 17:16:08

Eternal God, Jesus, Love

An ominous groan broke the night

Flowing across garden-earth

Mysterious trembling – shook the heavens

The Mighty One cast his shadow

Host on high ceased singing

Plead for mercy filled the air

From hidden chambers

Mystical darkness blocked the light

Trembling reached to a fever

Life was halted in every vein

Tears no longer streamed

His words crystallized

The evil served is the hunger of your heart

Corruption is beyond repair

Waters will not be used this time

My dissatisfaction will serve

Enough – heard in a soft whisper

Slashing light tore open the ground

Silence preserved

His voice was never heard again

No one lived in the garden – any more

It is finished.

Prayer Book Page 35

Fri, 16 Nov 2012 20:03:07

Eternal God, Jesus, Love

Beautiful glowing from beyond the sun

Caressed my spirit – mystical joy

Out of the light

Magnificent knowing

The truest joy of life

Learning – He does not desire to judge

Calling all to himself – promised joy

Unlike any other – sweetness for every soul

Eternal love inseparable

His joy embraces the depth of being

Living in his joy – eternal life

Every heart in his – rests in heaven

The purest joy engulfing

Nothing exists apart from Him

Jesus the only joy

Aware – the love he gives

Oneness of heart

Even as you do not exist

You live in him – joy eternal.

Prayer Book Page 36

Fri, 16 Nov 2012 20:05:07

Eternal God, Jesus, Love

My love – thunder fills my heart

Not simply noise

Coming from beyond the barrier

Between us

Chaotic storms trample the spirit

Seeding confusion and doubt

Fierce battles – plotting

Destruction – shattering prayers

With the gentle touch of your hand

My love- calm returns – restoration

Without the direction of your will

Peace – salvation – easily lost

In the peace – fragrance

Your love – devours the stench

Evil leaves on the battlefield of soul

Without you – no victory can flourish

My love –send forth you light

Dispel the thunder

Release the joy of you

End the violent attacks of evil

Our fragile souls need your protection

Prayer Book Page 37

Fri, 16 Nov 2012 20:06:24

Eternal God, Jesus, Love

Why is it - so many enter

My father's house

Empty of love and caring

Better they remain outside

Refraining from interfering

With the prosperity I give to those

Who believe in me

What can they expect – who are not of my body

Those who never come near me

Those who live a full lifetime

Without ever reaching for the truth

And have no desire to embrace me

The same who lash out at me

In all manner of sacrilege – but don't dare

To strike against their neighbor

For fear of retaliation

Is it possible – those who believe in nothing

End life with nothing

Waiting for them

While those who live in me

Are filled with the great joy of my love

Arriving in the place prepared

Escorted by my holy angels.

Prayer Book Page 38

Fri, 16 Nov 2012 20:07:50

Eternal God, Jesus, Love

My Lord, Jesus, so many

Of your children

Are weeping in the garden earth

Pain and suffering touches all

No one escapes the darkness

My love – has hell been released

To ravage and destroy the human spirit

You know we are not strong

To withstand the evil assaults

Send your holy angels to help

Save your children in the garden earth

Collect the tears – least they be squandered

Leaving to die – their love – in dried earth

In your fragrance – cleanse the pathways

Lift your children out of pain and weeping

Give birth today for faith in tomorrow

Let your love guide your children

Away from the fearful afflictions of evil

Into your life of peace and joy

Prayer Book Page 39

Thu, 29 Nov 2012 19:43:57

Eternal God, Jesus, Love

My Lord – my friend is gone

A very good friend he was

Coming to my home very often

He had no place to go

Sleeping nights in the streets

Curled up under plastic

Soaked to the skin

My friend never asked for anything

Each moment shared whatever was there

His smile was precious

For a long time he did not show

It turned – he was gone

Never speaking about his illness

Many days and nights – I wept

Quietly for him

His room is still there

Neat – clean – waiting for him

Just in case the bell rings

And he walks in

I pray for rain - pretending to go out and search for him

My love – embrace my friend

Lift him up – into your kingdom

Fill him with your magnificent grace

In a brief moment – let my friend know

I miss him.

Prayer Book Page 40

Mon, 03 Dec 2012 16:39:03

Eternal God, Jesus, Love

That man over there

Having considerable difficulty

Not sure what it is – he did not say

No probing – better to have distance

His praying is considerable – constant

My Savior – He begins

I pray for your grace of divine healing – LOVE

I pray for your grace of divine healing – MERCY

I pray for your grace of divine healing – COMPASSION

I pray for your grace of divine healing – FORGIVENESS

Through each hour you are before me

Your suffering on the cross – in my heart

Consuming my pain – I live in you my Savior

Knowing in the threads of our suffering

We are bound forever – one

Each day ends – as it begins

My spirit reaching for you – crucified

The song in my heart – unquenched

Suffering continues

I live – In your magnificent grace

Prayer Book Page 41

Thu, 06 Dec 2012 14:59:43

Eternal God, Jesus, Love

How long my Lord

Will I walk in this darkness

My spirit thirsts for your light

When will you end this empty wandering

Fill my soul

With your splendor and grandeur

End the meaningless ways of self

Better to understand your words

Let your breath carry my life

Forever caressed

Seeking no other sweetness

Purify me in the depths of your

Magnificent love –

Passion – Crucifixion – death

On the cross lift me to life

In the Resurrection promise

Death defeated

Eternal life – triumphant

To live forever

In the sweetness of your love

Prayer Book Page 42

Mon, 10 Dec 2012 19:02:15

Eternal God, Jesus, Love,

The joy of you held me

In the sweetness

Of your love - I lived subdued – quiet

Awakening to your gentle voice

Perception corrected

A peace that only you can give

My joy – complete – flourished

How long ago was it

In your embrace

I stopped calling you – my Lord

And began calling you

My love – O yes, my Love

You captured me

Now the full space of my heart

Belongs to only you

We are bound together in a place

Known as – forever

Nothing can be corrected – measured

Tomorrow ends now – in our space

Joy – precious gift – consuming

Relentless your pursuit

I am dissolved in the joy of you

Prayer Book Page 43

Sun, 06 Jan 2013 13:31:49

Eternal God, Jesus, Love

My love – this day – my offering

Pain and suffering – to blend

With your agony on the cross

Know the measure of my love

As I struggle to comprehend

Your love for me

When the hour arrives

Bringing your angel near

To lift me into your divinity

Let the man rest as nothing

Rather than having him live again away from you

Untouched by spiritual flowering

Separation from you is endless death

A void without fragrance

Of your breath

Knowing nothing- being nothing

Simply a shell living to die

There is one way – the narrow gate

The way of truth – you have paid the fee

My love – your cross – eternal life

Precious gift – to me

Prayer Book Page 44 - For Someone In Need

Tue, 22 Jan 2013 21:09:01

Holy Lord Jesus, God of love and life,

This day in humble prayer – we plead

Accept into your sacred heart

One suffering – in need of you

Be inclined Jesus, we pray

Extend your love, mercy and

Compassion to (name)

In your grace end pain and suffering

To the praise and glory of thy holy name,

Spirit, and in the glory of our

Heavenly Father

Amen

Prayer Book Page 45

Wed, 30 Jan 2013 21:04:34

Eternal God, Jesus, Love

My Love, you see how

The weight of my afflictions

Crushes my spirit

Reaching for you – My Love

My consolation

Lifts me – not to be free

From my suffering – but to hold fast

Every pain – into oneness with you

You alone – Jesus – can make sense

And give meaning to suffering

There are times – through you

A great joy springs forth

From suffering – when shared

In your sacred heart

Jesus, you are the difference

Between suffering alone

For nothing – in angry darkness

And continuing gracefully

In your magnificent love on the cross

Embraced in life and peace

Prayer Book Page 46

Sat, 09 Feb 2013 14:13:35

Eternal God, Jesus, Love
The heavens are being filled
With the cries of millions
Very difficult to understand – 55 million

All indications show - 100 million
Is not far off - then what
How long will the evil continue
Soon there will be no space left
To hold them and their tears

Heard from your lips my love
"Forgive them they know not what they do"
A different cross now stands – outside of heaven
Before Almighty God – crying out
"Do not forgive them – they know exactly what they are doing"

Take into your holy spirit, Jesus
These millions torn from life
Let them rest in the comfort of your love

For such grievous things
Where can we go
Only to your cross – to find you my love
Believing Jesus you will one day
Make all things right.

Prayer Book Page 47

Tue, 19 Feb 2013 19:35:54

Eternal God, Jesus, Love

There was one beside me

Complaining loudly about so much pain

Over and over blaming you – my love

Tried very hard to enlighten him

You Jesus are not the cause of his suffering

Such a thing is contrary

To your being – the purest love

Why do I suffer? He asked over and over

For Jesus to cause your suffering

Contradicts his magnificent love

Given to all – on the cross

Your suffering comes from evil

Desperate to separate you from Jesus

Desperate to destroy your love for God

Evil inflicts you with terrible suffering

Embrace Jesus on the cross

Offer him your suffering

Defeat – through Jesus – the evil

That hurts you

Rest in Jesus – in his magnificent love

Prayer Book Page 48

Thu, 21 Feb 2013 18:58:24

Eternal God, Jesus, Love

The Lady in white appeared again

In the glow of your sacred heart

Written there – love – in gold letters

Silver tears in her eyes

Calling out – Mother of love

Prayers are taken away

Weeping is near

Longing is heavy

Desire – rest in his arms

Mother take me there

Let him know of my love

Together – embracing – complete

Healing spirit – Mother – True

Prayers live anew

With you to stay

No more wandering

In fruitless darkness

Give the dream again

Mother – lady in white

Ultimate grace – unending

Take me to him

Mother – eternal

Voice of my soul

Prayer Book Page 49

Sun, 10 Mar 2013 17:46:10

Eternal God, Jesus, Love

Lifted in spirit – to the edge

The barrier – keeping us separated

No passing beyond

Reaching to hold – impossible

Whence comes this light

Shattering the barrier

Exposing a lifeless garden

In the light – life renews

Joy embraces joy

Voices – chanting - defy the barrier

Now – in the light - rendered meaningless

Radiant – he stands – in himself – light

Wounded – yet magnificent love – offered

In him – the barrier is defeated

He calls the lifted – follow him

Share the victory

Beings of light – escort

Salvation – joy – elevation

Out of darkness – the kingdom

His love – no beginning – no end

Prayer Book Page 50

Sat, 16 Mar 2013 17:20:18

Eternal God, Jesus, Love

Through everyday – I cry for you

There in my joy is found

In the depth of my pain

I know you are reaching for me

Through long night hours

My suffering increases

There in my joy

I know – you are reaching for me

My joy – my love

Reaches for your healing love

Your merciful love

Your compassionate love

Your forgiving love

Racing through the heavens

Glorious among the angels

In the embrace of your holy spirit

Through the breach – into your kingdom

Free to be- forever

Reaching – ended

Now – holding onto you – my love

Prayer Book Page 51

Fri, 22 Mar 2013 18:34:26

Eternal God, Jesus, Love

My Love – My place now

With you – nothing needed

Together at long last

No yesterday – tomorrow

Instant now – eternal

Light – pure –giving

Life – joy – immeasurable

You my love are joy

This place – prepared for me

By you – before I was born

In you – my spirit thrives

Your glory – my love

That I may also be

This is not in any way

A state of mind

For in my resurrection

I am complete in you my love

Prayer Book Page 52

Sun, 24 Mar 2013 15:09:24

Eternal God, Jesus, Love

My love, the Lady in white returned

Dream or vision – mystical encounter

Beauty – stunning – in golden light

Consciousness staggered – lost is my being

Before the magnificent Lady, my voice or mind

Moving to the rim of the light

Mother – my only word

How is it you call me Mother

The truth reveals itself – my heart

The child – Mother –would you like

To hold my son – weeping I cannot

Reply – reaching – he is in my arms

My spirit trembles

Our eyes embrace – great gift of love

Mother calls - He looks up his little hand

Holds my face – He is back in her arms

I must go now – where I ask

Heaven waits and calls

The Journey begins – the child smiles

Sending affection

Wait Mother take me with you

Not now – your time is not fulfilled

The child smiles – power in his eyes

Mother's journey continues

I will return in a while - pray

Mother is gone – waking is not easy

Prayer Book Page 53

Thu, 28 Mar 2013 19:07:29

Eternal God, Jesus, Love
Lifted in spirit across a great valley
Garden – earth deep in profound darkness
Stopping only to witness a tiny speck of light
Holding eternity in the center of the darkness
Being there to witness the tiny speck of light
A lifetime needed to arrive
The closer in approach great power known
From the tiny speck of light
Roaring through the cold and lifeless darkness
Bursting forth shattering explosion of light
Consuming the darkness
Exhausted unable to reach up I remain
At his feet yearning to hold him
On his cross – feeling the power
Of his life giving light
This one I love – his cross to share
He reached and in his will I was there
My arms around him – eyes embraced
Through time love unknown – almost unbearable
You have to leave – was given
Refusing I said no
I cannot leave him
I cannot let go of him
You must leave – I said no again
Holding this one I love even stronger
He is my life this is my cross
He is mine I cannot leave him
With the darkness consumed
Life blossomed in the garden – earth
I refused to leave him
Dissolve me into nothing in his grace
We are one forever – unending love
He is mine – I am his there is no going back
To what was.

Prager Book Page 54

Fri, 05 Apr 2013 19:41:13

Eternal God, Jesus, Love

Quietly to speak my love

I pray you will live in me

Never more to be the man lost in yesterday

That I may hold you in every moment

Let the blood you shed fill my spirit

Carry me beyond the way of mortality

Live in me Jesus, your heart – a place to live

Take my heart – a place to live

Keep me in the light of your magnificent love

In continuous communion

Live in me Jesus, never to thirst again

Drink living waters, the purity of you

Your cross within, radiantly alive

In your mercy, I become you

In your mercy you become me

Live in me, Jesus, illumine my will

If it is not your own, tear it out of my spirit

Cast it into the fire, as it denies me

Your eyes blinding me

Live in me Jesus, my resurrection

How wonderful I can live beyond now

In ways divine – in you Jesus

Time never ends – it does not exist

Prayer Book Page 55

Tue, 09 Apr 2013 17:40:37

Eternal God, Jesus, Love

You send every soul into life

Through your holy will

From your hands

All arrive bearing the seed of purity

In time so many of the pure

Obtain to an insatiable curiosity

Towards the seed of darkness

Tending to lose the light given

They slip into the wrong embrace

Lethal entanglements surface

The seed of purity cannot flourish

Buried in desires – that are lies

Without light – purity withers

Blind spirits – groping in darkness

Unable to find grace

Unable to dispel the darkness – to embrace the light

Yet freedom returns – life in the seed of purity

Born again – holy will – eternal God.

Prayer Book Page 56

Thu, 18 Apr 2013 19:22:18

Eternal God, Jesus, Love

My love, the lady in white

Returned, dream or vision – no matter

So beautiful – I am stunned

Each time I see her

Suffering became painful – within

Beautiful lady crying

My spirit trembled – asking

Why, dear lady, why

There is no heart that cares

No heart willing to carry my tears

No heart waiting for the love of my tears

My heart leaped – offering – pleading

For the tears of the beautiful lady

My spirit stopped breathing

Tears of love came to me

The beautiful lady reached

I remained in suspension

Stay forever here – my prayer

Glowing tears – alive in my heart

Mystical peace holding me

For the longest time

Joy unknown – given – magnificent love

Prayer Book Page 57

Mon, 22 Apr 2013 18:57:35

Eternal God, Jesus, Love

My love, waited for you

Through long night hours

Prayer filled hours – my spirit

Longing, hoping, filled with desire

Once in your embrace

Reaching deep into your heart

My own heart enriched

Your magnificent love – hope fulfilled

Your comfort – always ready

To embrace every heart – with desire

Unsparing – unconcealed love

The joy of you – beyond understanding

My heart keeping all you freely give

My love, I hold your words

Heart pierced in anger

Brought forth an eternal

Flow of love – precious blood

For all who seek life

Unending – in you

Prayer Book Page 58

Mon, 29 Apr 2013 19:14:26

Eternal God, Jesus, Love

My Love, for many days I have searched

Ever so seriously, for a special gift

For you, from my heart

In your mystical ways, my love

The beautiful light came

I watched as your hands reached

Taking from me my heart

Filled with a life time of love

Filled with a lifetime of gratitude

Filled with a lifetime of desire

To be one with you

Then it began, as you held my heart

A beating within me

You own heart - I saw them t together

Beating as one - My insignificance and

Your glorious majesty – embracing - consuming

My spirit moved to the side

Alive in the power of your holy will

Please my love – Keep my heart

Leave your own - Let eternity begin

The fragrance of you sustains me

Leaving me without any knowledge

Of myself – only you Jesus

Desire fulfilled – in your magnificent love

Prayer Book Page 59

Wed, 05 Jun 2013 19:26:26

Eternal God, Jesus, Love

My love, there emerges from within

A mystery, one that can come only

Through your direction

Awareness through a lifetime

Has taught me about myself

A physical being

That in time finally ends

Now my love, a new issue

Somehow from the beginning

Unable to blossom – you put it there

Understanding non existent

Time to be reaching – time to know

How my love to embrace

The old man was told

He would die very soon

Oh, no he said, that cannot be

For his divinity

Is forever the other half

Of me

My love, send your grace

To reveal who I am

Understanding the whole of me

That I am too, Divinity

Prayer Book Page 60

Tue, 11 Jun 2013 21:47:28

Eternal God, Jesus, Love
My Love, not far off
Is the cry - for mercy
Dampen loneliness of spirit
My love – mercy in its ending

Terrible is the longing for you
My love, this heart is meaningless
Life's love remains empty
Longing for grace – peace

Now heavy is the way without light
That which can no longer be carried
End moments without you

Desire becomes a heavy cross
Crushing the spirit
Unyielding love reaching
Beyond the loneliness
Being apart from you

My love – is there any merit
To wash away exhaustion
Let me be one with you – now
Bring an end to relentless desire
Every heart filled
With desire for
Oneness with you, Jesus
Know the desolation
Of separation
From you, purest love

Prayer Book Page 61

Tue, 02 Jul 2013 22:37:38

Eternal God, Jesus, Love
My Love, the press of shadows
Heavy against the spirit – pain in every
Space – eyes reaching for you
Speaking words of love

There is unspoken sorrow – rivers of blood
Little ones murdered through choice
My Love – prayers are pleading
Send your holy angels to gather the slain

Holy spirit is weeping – brutal ending
Of Life – sanctified in his divine breath
My Love – prayers offered for tortured wombs
Seem to fall into the slaughter
Heavenly choirs rendered silent
Lamenting screams – innocents dying

My Love – the prayer – remains unknown
Having come from you
My love to repeat every day
Gives life to those broken away

Prayer Book Page 62

Wed, 03 Jul 2013 15:13:45

Eternal God, Jesus, Love
My Love, the Lady in White
Returned the other day
When I see her – I cannot speak

When I see her I am held
In fragrant quiet – so sweet
Stillness fills my soul – my spirit
My thought is one – to stay with
The beautiful lady in white

Do not leave me, take me with you
The endless longing of my heart
To be with you or be nothing
In your peace dear lady
Let time exhaust itself – I remain with you

Let my prayer reach you
Beautiful lady in white
I seek nothing to possess
Only to be in your embrace
Beyond forever

Give my love for you – meaning
Let the grace of you
Beautiful lady in white
Fill and contain my spirit

Prayer Book Page 63

Wed, 17 Jul 2013 10:35:48

Eternal God, Jesus, Love
My Love, this day my reaching for you
Is very intense – you must be near
As my spirit is very restless

There is no peace away from you
My Love – like being stranded
Being alone is sharp – painful
Each new day – embraced by you
Must be – thanks giving

Where, my love will prayers
Carry the spirit – eternal ground
Beyond the temporary – fleeting moments
Life slips into channels of disturbing
Restless encounters

Grateful my love – thanks is not enough
Yet you never complain at the meagerness
Of my offering for the grace you give
What gift can I give that at least
Lets you know of my love and gratitude
That you live each day – in me

Prayer Book Page 64

Wed, 31 Jul 2013 22:54:45

Eternal God, Jesus, Love
My love, you must know how dreadful
Interior darkness can be
Where nothing extends
From or to the spirit
Intense prayer must engulf
The spirit until threads of grace
Return – and bind the soul in peace

My love, in you the way
Is never empty or barren
So much to reach for – one thorn
At least – who can attain to all
The weight of which would be crushing

To understand is not the jewel
The rose remains beautiful and desired
Understood or not
Better to embrace and hold the beauty
Filling the spirit - fragrance divine

The greatest mystery – is you my love
The reach of your love
Such a great evil – rejection of you
Your magnificent love of the cross
Yet, the rose - the fragrance my love
Live eternal – reaching
For every yearning heart

Prayer Book Page 65

Wed, 31 Jul 2013 22:51:56

Eternal God, Jesus, Love
Speak again your words
Something good will be
Let there be light – so good
To fill and illuminate my spirit

My Love, speak again your words
Create my spirit new
Out of your mouth – your words
Bring me forth out of nothing
The same as you created all things

My love let your words
Speak my name – to live forever
In your voice

My love – living in you
Forever   fresh and beautiful
Speak my name – anew I am born
To live forever in your glory

My love   let your words be again
In your light forever
My spirit – no beginning – no end
Your words keep me
To be with you – magnificent love

Prayer Book Page 66

Eternal God, Jesus, Love
The way is long – difficult
Many times – the cross is too heavy
Not picked up – left behind
Yet – the path remains arduous

My love, apart from you
Life is empty – no graces
Loss of embraces weakens the spirit
Darkness swells like a great ocean
Leaving the spirit wondering
Will light ever return

My love, your nearness brings warmth
Doubt – confusion taken away
Your peace captures anxiety
My love – you are the only way
Joy – The truth of you

My love – what is it that causes you
To seek my heart – so relentlessly
Even as I know – I am nothing
I flee into your arms
Separating myself from all things
Praying – gratefully
To remain in your embrace
Forever

Prayer Book Page 67

Fri, 30 Aug 2013 16:03:55

Eternal God, Jesus, Love
My spirit was lifted to a place unknown
Leaving me in front of you
Your brightness so great
Darkness held the eyes of spirit

Slowly you softened your power
Allowing completion for my spirit
There in your light – consumed
I was no longer me
My being merged with you
My love eternal

Please my love – let me stay
Wrapped in your light
Face to face in the river of your love
In your presence – union complete

Let me stay – one in you
Your face is mine
In your being I am now – forever
Let me stay my love
In your light – eternal life

Prayer Book Page 68

Mon, 09 Sep 2013 13:56:03

Eternal God, Jesus, Love
Many hours pass so quickly
Falling into deep prayerful moments
Each moment so fragile
Breaking and fracturing
Bearing Fruit of emptiness

What can it mean?
This way of things
Where darkness wakens
That which longs for rest

Send now my love
That tiny point of light
Surging with life
Let your love create again
Life beyond ending- holding you
Each prayer recovering its moment
In you – only you – life is true

Waiting here – for you –my love
Reaching through empty ways
Your embrace – peace – love – life
Now I – in turn my love hold you

Prayer Book Page 69

Wed, 18 Sep 2013 21:43:14

Eternal God, Jesus, Love
The Lady in white returned
Beyond description – beautiful
How or why – left alone
She is as she is – magnificent

My love, the beautiful Lady
Smiled – wrapping me into your name
Profound peace embraced
The universe of my being
In the expanse of eternal light
Fragrance of absolute purity
Flooded the endless existence of my spirit

My love – if you do not reach
I will remain only light
Beginning and ending – joined

Please, my love, ask the beautiful Lady
Not to leave – least I fall into the sorrow
Of darkness

My love – let the magnificent
You joyously gave to the lady in white
Remain beautiful – holding my spirit
Forever

Prayer Book Page 70

Sat, 28 Sep 2013 16:03:51

Eternal God, Jesus, Love

Trying to hide – my spirit yields

Intensely warm - separation

Immanent – but for the touch

Of your hand – suffering stayed

When you are near – my love – I tremble

So powerful your thirst

Yearning is for dissolution

Only love can remain - before you

You are here – light of you

A burning rises in the heart

Life – extends – heat of the flame

Living love – splendid union

If you leave – my love

I cannot live – emptiness too exhausting

Your grace – place me in you

Separation – eternal weeping

My Love – my spirit reaches every day

In prayerful love – you are

My one desire – nothing before

Or after you – no purpose – only you

My one love – seeking to leave

Everything – last breath in your arms

My love

Prayer Book Page 71

Sun, 06 Oct 2013 14:50:59

Eternal God, Jesus, Love
Such joy, my love when
You lifted my spirit
Leaving me standing in a
Great valley of the splendid
Garden – earth – where all is new

Fearless – watching the great
Arch – angel freeing the blue skies
Feeling divine love embracing
Every blade of the lush green fields

My love – your name suspends all
Nothing moves – until your light
Breaches the silence
Life blossoms – in your breath
Let me remain in the endless way

My love – take me to the rim
Of the garden – earth
To join the angels singing
Into the depths of new life
To be in the final vision

Beyond all things – my love
Only you are always with me
No matter the pain or suffering
My spirit rests in the sweetness of your love

Prayer Book Page 72

Wed, 30 Oct 2013 20:32:25

Eternal God, Jesus, love
My love, you lifted me again
In spirit – to the edge of the great valley
Of life – showing me a painful day approaching
Merciful love – extended reaching
Fails to recover – smiles vanishing
Afflictions rising – eyes only tears

My love – so much suffering
Such dismay hindering
Seldom smiles creating
My love – embrace them

In the glow of your compassion
Each cross is carried
My suffering is worse
Passing – I cannot heal them

My love – mend broken hearts
Free them – end their sorrow
Your love – your grace – comfort
Lead them into your heart
Rest in the sanctuary – the joy of you.

My Love – beyond the pain – only you
Beyond the darkness – only you
The way of hope – only you
The way of mercy – only you

Prayer Book Page 73

Mon, 04 Nov 2013 11:09:48

Eternal God, Jesus, Love
My love, for so many years the
Struggle has been – what to
Offer you in thanksgiving for all
You have done for me

Something that will please you – My love
Something that will go beyond the
Shallow and simple – thank you
My love reaching for you – for so many years
Has not been easy – searching for a gift for you

My love – this simple little box
Is my offering – please open slowly
When you look inside – you will see nothing
The very essence of my being – my nothingness
My offer to you – my love – is my nothingness
You glory – holds all that I am – nothing
My love – keep the box open – allow
The grace of your love – to fill my being
Giving significance to my offering

My love – throughout all time – my spirit
Weeps for your embrace
Please eternal God, my love – Jesus
Let my being – my nothingness – blossom in your
Magnificent love

Prayer Book Page 74

Sun, 22 Dec 2013 18:53:41

Eternal God, Jesus, Love
My love, there comes to mind
Something to speak to you about
My love never, have you turned
Away from my spirit reaching for you

During such times – when I am summoned
To pray – the eyes of my spirit open
Embracing a soft blue light

Through the intensity of my awareness
Suffering overtakes my being
Thrusting me into terrible pain

The weight of great loneliness
Blankets my spirit – concealing the light
Revealing that no matter how close
You allow me to approach
I learn painfully – I cannot possess you
The ultimate joy and glory

Knowing such a lonely separation
During intense prayer
I am forced to retreat – to collapse
Weeping – suffering – knowing
How poor I really am
My peace – my love – my friend
No matter what happens – I will never let go

Prayer Book Page 75

Sat, 11 Jan 2014 16:58:14

Eternal God, Jesus Love
My love, the purity of all grace
Returned – the lady in white
In dream or in vision – engulfed me
In great joy – when I look upon her
How magnificent it is to behold
Her Glory

There is something left to do
Her words – it is time to enter
The fires of purifying love
To be held until the fires are completed

Living in the fires of purification
Is absolute ecstasy – never to know again
The nature of anything – except you – my love
Purifying my spirit in the cleansing fires
Of you love – reaching for the final vision
Union throughout all eternity – my joy

In the flames of unending purification
My spirit – in ecstasy – blossoms into
Divine fragrance – joyfully embracing you
My love –eternal – life - freedom

Prayer Book Page 76

Mon, 27 Jan 2014 08:51:00

Eternal God, Jesus Love,
My Love, how wonderful to learn
Your light is in every soul
At the very moment of being

We learn no one is born alone
Multitudes of angels – singing in choir
Welcome each new cry
Bringing your light – joy throughout
The kingdom – each new song

To think – my love – the very substance
In each of us – from your hand
Eternal life – breaths at each beginning
That you love us so much

In you alone, there is eternal life
Beyond understanding – caretakers
Arrive – to carry you love
In your light – what is to be
Comes together – now
Known as friends – you and me

Prayer Book Page 77

Fri, 28 Feb 2014 15:24:40

Eternal God, Jesus, Love
My love, last night a child cried
For a long time – I surprised myself
Knowing the man never cried
The child watched as the man
Went to war – Gone forever

My love, a child cried last night
For a very long time – memories unsorted
In tears calling the man home
Unchanged – the child would know him

That would never be, the child and
The man would never embrace again
Even now he was not the same
There was a space now
In the war the man changed
Dying to his changes

The child lives free – knowing
The man and child in all of us
One lives – one dies
Two living in all of us
The man went to war
There were no surprise – the changes
Not expected – were real

Prayer Book Page 78

Eternal God, Jesus, Love
My Love, you opened the eyes of my spirit
Again – reaching for you – such desire
Overwhelming the shadows – pain inflicted

Desire – reaching for life
Unable to embrace – there in a
Magnificent love – the purest love
You gave completion to desire

My Love – Beyond the limits
Of this garden – carry me
Let me vanish in the way of your grace
Without you there is no meaning
Remaining outside of you
And beyond your magnificent love
Desire no longer lives - only darkness

My Love – Let your desire reach for me
Enable my longing – in your gift of love
Let me be there with you
In your embrace – desire fulfilled
My love – my beginning – without ending
You – my eternal purpose
My love – in union – breathing
The Godly breath of life

Prayer Book Page 79

Mon, 24 Mar 2014 22:32:09

Eternal God, Jesus, Love
My Love, so joyful moments with you
Grace fills the spirit –peace – loving embrace

In your light –seeing you teaching
Your words reaching me – the prayer
Saying – "Give us this day our daily bread"

Angels carried me to the "supper"
You spoke again my love
Giving bread from your hand
Saying – "Take this bread and eat it" "For this is my body"

In those moments, my love the path
From – "Our daily bread"
To – "This is my body"
Filled with your light and I understood

You my love are my Daily Bread
The bread of life – within I hold you
From the cross – my daily bread

The mystery remains
My love – please open the path again
In your light – my love – my Daily Bread

Prayer Book Page 80

Sun, 30 Mar 2014 22:00:42

Eternal God, Jesus, Love
My love, the deep of night
Broke open – my eyes reached for the
Tiny spec of light – coming from
A great distance – with a great roar

The eyes of my spirit opened in the light
Of you my love – on a great cross
Weeping upon seeing every wound
I was warned – feeling every wound

The lady in white interceded – sparing me
Lest I perish at your feet – although relieved
No desire for the garden remained
Better to die in you – live in you

An angel whispered, "Say a prayer"
My being roused, "My love, I offer
Every pain and suffering of my life as a gift of my love,
For your magnificent love on the cross"

The angel whispered again, "He is leaving – pray
My love, please purify my spirit in the agony
Of your passion, crucifixion and death on the cross"
Heard in the deep of the night,
"I will take your prayers with me"
The eyes of my spirit closed – the deep held me

Prayer Book Page 81

Wed, 16 Apr 2014 20:00:11

Eternal God, Jesus, Love

My Love – you were so near

The breath of your love

Swept over me – warm – filing

Great joy captured my spirit

Peace swelled like an advancing tide

Prostrate before you – my love

Begging to share every wound

All of heave has been pierced

At your feet – holding the cross

Of salvation – reaching your

Magnificent love

As angels mourn – He who has been pierced

Greatest desire   hold you   your love

Look into your eyes – yearning – hoping

My Love – away the pain – longing

That only such desire can bring

To join you – being one – on the wood

In dissolution – all is done

Thriving in your light – completion

There at your feet – receiving life

You my love brought here

Eternal union

Prayer Book Page 82

Sun, 27 Apr 2014 16:07:06

Eternal God, Jesus, Love
My Love, the garden is held
In grave danger – return my love
Save that which you have created
So very beautiful – fearful
Will be the cry – why have you
Abandoned us

My Love – send caressing angels
To provide the light – love – to all
Who reach for you – living hope
To forbid the mortal way

Those who hated – shouted loudly
Against you – death – their claim
Holy angels wept – seeing your
Magnificent love – pierced with
Thorns and nails – suffering in the
Depths of anger

Reaching for your embrace
Forgive the way of this one
Let Him keep his arms around you
He knew not what he was doing

Prayer Book Page 83

Fri, 02 May 2014 19:59:23

Eternal God, Jesus, Love
My love, so many times
It happens, prayers seem empty
Not enough to reach you – left
To grasp only emptiness
Filling spirit with suffocating
Loneliness – denying spirit
Of your magnificent love –

So difficult not being held in your embrace
Spirit lives in a cold space – suffering
Unbearable loneliness
Dare to pray again – reaching for
The warmth of you – leaving spirit
To weep in a great joy

My love, how can spirit survive
Being separated from you – nothing lives
Shower your mercy here – give life
To living in your way – through heavy hours

The tiny spec of light so far away
Begins its journey – giving love to the
Waiting in an explosion of brilliant
White light – filling the spirit – life and love

Prayer Book Page 84

Eternal God, Jesus, Love
My Love, praying throughout the night
Spirit rises to ask
Is it possible you would
Consider coming here for a visit

As you are seen on the cross
Let your embrace lengthen
And hear in thanksgiving – souls
Speaking of your love – our love
Thank you for the gift of everyday

The gift of profound understanding
Lady in White in
Mother of God – Giving all eternity
In miraculous union

Visit for a while my love
Let us hold you – looking into your eyes
Be one with you – spirit crossing
The line – holding you – in union – one

There is no other purpose – to be
No other reason to live
If not in you – spirit breathing
Weeping in joy - consumed in you
My love – spirit lives in peace
In you – my love – the only truth

Prayer Book Page 85

Sun, 08 Jun 2014 16:54:39

Eternal God, Jesus, Love

My Love, these several days and nights

Have been unusually heavy

Your grace served to soften the way

Poor ones – continued on – ever quietly

Each soul approaching – understands

The serious need for your embrace

Knowing you are the only one who can give

True peace and joy – living in you

Spirit being enraptured – in you alone

My love – prayer calls to you

Please do not remain beyond my finger tips

Leaving me unable to take hold of you

And draw you into my heart

While my longing reaches into forever

You feel so far away – often at days end

Then – there you are – so close beside me

Everyday my love, spirit begs in your glory

Live in me – Let me share every moment

Prayer turns away the emptiness

Until the joy of you sparkles – spirit is held

Spirit cannot live – away from you the only good

Keep me there, my love, in your wounds

The only truth – eternal life

Prayer Book Page 86

Sun, 29 Jun 2014 13:46:29

Eternal God, Jesus, Love

My Love, how is it you have

Looked upon such a lowly creature

To fill spirit with such great joy

My Love, so many times

I ask myself – why

Surely – on my own I have done

Nothing to receive such wonderful

Gifts from you – out of the depths of

Your magnificent love

You leave me exhausted trying

To find a way to adequately

Say thank you – even as I know

These words will never reach

The levels of your gracious embraces

My Love, my heart will never rest

Until it finds your heart of love

Then my love – dissolve all that

I am in you – never to be

Separated from you – to live in

Such sorrow – knowing such

A thing has - happened - never

To see the light of life –

In you – life eternal

Prayer Book Page 87

Wed, 16 Jul 2014 21:50:30

Eternal God, Jesus, Love
My Love, woke this morning
To hear the earth sobbing
Horrible sounds of great suffering

A giant bird, made of steal
Flew over the garden – hiding the sun
Leaving a great explosion – filling the
Garden with terrible agony

My prayers flew like tiny birds
Bringing tiny lights – to pierce the
Darkness – protesting against the devastation
My Love, what can be done – to save
Our garden – from the grip of evil

Return in humble prayer to my father
Love him – not evil – he alone can save you
Mankind lives in the arms of evil, no soul
Can come to me – unless forgiven by my father

Pray long hours in seclusion – and repentance
Lest the earth cry and tremble in a savage way
As the hordes gather to the north – gathering
To prepare afflictions against the garden
My love – save us from pending peril
List to me – "Watch for the days of my Mother"

Prayer Book Page 88

Fri, 01 Aug 2014 08:31:44

Eternal God, Jesus, Love
My Love, all night – thunder
Drenching rain – darkness unrelenting
Then the dawn – your sweeping hand
Swirled the darkness disappearing
In the pursuing sun

The warming light – embracing
Relieving pain – loves entitlements
How sweet the way
Walking well without sandals

My love – so generous – filling
Spirit with such love
Can't go on anymore
Here – ways are so painful

Free my spirit, my love
No more wandering
In ways so empty – aimless
Let the next moment – recline
Even in the tiniest way
Knowing life is forever
In the blessed truth of you
My love – only you – my love
Let me carry the cross with you

Prayer Book Page 89

Eternal God, Jesus, Love
My Love, I see the sorrows
Arriving with each new day
Continuing through the ending
Spiritual pain and suffering
Not being able to see you

Then, my love, there is the sorrow
Of not being able to hear your voice
The end of days approaches
Bringing suffering in the failure
To hold and keep your magnificent love
On the cross-seeing the worst of all
Unbearable pain – not being forgiven
By you, my love

Is your heart in a place too far
Send the sweet child of purity
To bring the light of your love
Let this heart begin life anew

You are they mystery – my love
Enabling this creature – empty of grace
To speak without fear
To the highest glory

Prayer Book Page 90

Thu, 14 Aug 2014 20:03:01

Eternal God, Jesus, Love
My love, the Lady in White returned
Dream or vision – my love – unknown

Magnificently beautiful – I am frozen
Looking at the light with in the glowing Lady
Held in stillness – her beauty
Magnifies my being

The Lady speaks, not sure how I hear
Words come and live within me
"You have been given a great friend
Remain loyal, lest the Father recall my Son
Leaving you empty of his love
Heaven – through his love – is for all mankind
Yet, heaven suffers – seeing so many
Turning away from perfect love"

My spirit is moved to sadness
Listening to the Lady
Her weeping is all embracing
Pleading for prayers for her children
Tell them to return – to the sounds
Of nails being driven – return to words
Forgiving – return to the blood of everlasting life
Return to my Son and his promise
Lest there never again – be peace in the garden

Prayer Book Page 91

Thu, 28 Aug 2014 19:13:11

Eternal God, Jesus, Love
My love, these times weigh
Heavily against me, how is it
Almighty God you let a lowly
Creature like me hold onto you
Taking the time I need
To find peace – rest until
I am able to steady myself

My spirit weeps seeking
Gifts to give you – my poverty
Is exposed in my offerings
My love and gratitude is
All I have to offer – while spirit
Seeks purification in the depths
Of your passion, crucifixion
And death on the cross

My love – the hours pass with
Inconsolable pain and suffering
May I hold on to you longer
To know the healing grace of you
In union – peace and love
Unable to let go

Prayer Book Page 92

Sun, 21 Sep 2014 08:40:05

Eternal God, Jesus, Love
My love, these are not complaints
But sorrows I carry deep in my heart
Surely, my love, you know of these

I have never seen you.
Never heard your voice
Never looked into your eyes
To tell you, I love you
Never been able to touch you
To share the depth of your agony

Never have I been able
To stand beside you
Hold you in my arms

Never has there been
Such a severe loneliness
In spirit – so close to ending

In that hour when my eyes close
And my lips are sealed
Never again to speak – I love you
I will know clearly
My love – my faith in you
Is eternal

Prayer Book Page 93

Mon, 06 Oct 2014 21:14:55

Eternal God, Jesus, Love
My Love, reaching for you
Almost in desperation, the pain
Adds up larger than a mountain

Your very name brings comfort
Peace, renewal of spirit
Still I search for gifts for you
To show gratitude extending – my heart

Please my love – come back
End the evil destroying mankind
Send your saints to give their goodness
Fill the earth with goodness

My love, please do not stop hearing our crying
Your mercy so wanting – needed
Save mankind – seeking evil
In horrible eagerness

Keep us awake in your love
Lest we sleep forever
In the darkness
My love – mercy upon us
Only in you does respite
From suffering come to us

Prayer Book Page 94

Sun, 12 Oct 2014 14:09:44

Eternal God, Jesus, Love
My Love, my days have reached
Longing for a special grace
The grace of silence for my soul
To live in heavenly quiet free of
All noise and distractions

One time the silence was so powerful
My spirit shook – disturbing the
Quiet in a profound way

My love, loosen me from all distractions
Noise that steals from the quiet
Leaving only shambles – empty of love

The grace of silence – rendering every
Thought not of you - foolish nonsense
The heart reaches for quiet spirit
Your being – forgive empty meaningless excess

How to possess – holy silence
The blessing and purity – your quiet
To take you into spirit
Life is you – in quiet – in silence – loving

My love –live in me – silence – quiet - pure
Let spirt hear the whispers
Of your holy angels

Prayer Book Page 95

Thu, 16 Oct 2014 11:46:16

Eternal God, Jesus, Love
My Love, how wonderful to
Wake from darkness of night
To the great joy of renewal
In you

No matter the aches and pains
The savage carnage in the garden
In the first light of day we
Find the splendid comfort of your love

The great joy of you, my love
Always there – waiting for us
To speak your name, offering our
Own imperfect love

Times past, words in spirit
Said, "Thank you for the new day"
Now spirit joyfully speaks
Thank you for my life – to engage
In prayer for so many suffering

There is no gift equal to the
Joy of you – giving life – from your spirit
But in the softness of your coming
The offer is made
Thank you, my love, for my life
All that it is and is not

Prayer Book Page 96

Mon, 20 Oct 2014 18:46:49

Eternal God, Jesus, Love
My Love, how wonderful
To discover joys of you
My greatest joy, my love
Is you
Spirit resting in your
Magnificent love on the cross

Each day knowing
The joy of your mercy
Singing with the angels
In the joy of your compassion

My love, surely I must
Consider the greatest joy
Is that you love me
In my nothingness

Beyond that is the purest joy
Mary, your Mother
Who leads all to you

Now then, my love, there is
The greatest joy of all
One you offer freely to all
Mankind
The everlasting joy of your resurrection

Prayer Book Page 97

Tue, 28 Oct 2014 14:28:05

Eternal God, Jesus, Love
My love, time to pray
For the so many – who are so sick

Please my love, look with great
Mercy and compassion on so many
Only you can provide comfort, consolation
Healing for so many suffering
Who cannot pray - or speak your name

There are times they cannot rise
Extend their arms to reach for you
My love, reach for them – embracing
Them – softening the terrible pain they endure
In your love – hold them

Reward their faith in you
Their love for you – keeps them
From despair – anger – surrender

My love, there is so much suffering
Cries of pain fill the hours
The only love – bringing hope – peace
Before so many find sleep in you
Peace and joyful rest in you
My love – hold them – so many sick

Prayer Book Page 98

Sun, 02 Nov 2014 14:10:13

Eternal God, Jesus, Love

In the first light of dawn

I wait for you, my love, to share

In the renewal of the garden

Eager to pray and stay with you

Through the long hours of day

Into sleepless moments of night

Continuous prayers to remain with you

Gathering the endless embrace

Of your magnificent love

Over there, just beyond the rim

Of the garden, a golden cross

Joining the ways of heaven

With those of a the garden

In the union of a great and

Beautiful light, the cross –gives

Life to all – in peace and love

Choirs of holy angels welcome

The arrival of a new dawn

Gathering around your cross

Receiving life in the light of you

Singing to your glory – peace and life

In your light – my love – I live –forever

Prayer Book Page 99

Sun, 23 Nov 2014 17:02:29

Eternal God, Jesus, Love
My love, on angels wings soaring
Across the great valley – filled with
Sparkling lights of the garden
Hope- supreme – anxious to arrive

Into the deepest reaches of heaven
Stopping in the center of the kingdom
Resting at the foot of a golden cross
Pulsating powerful – pure light – speaking
Life – into heavenly creatures and those
Thriving in the garden – your embrace is life

The angel must conceal me – in his wings
Closed – protecting against the power of the light
Providing warmth – peaceful love
Away from you – only darkness

Let me hide behind the golden cross
Never to return to the garden filled with
Pain and sadness – suffering in darkness
Let me hold your hands – feet – thorns
Never again to live without you
In the great union – my soul in you forever
I live in the sweet perfume
Of your love

Prayer Book Page 100

Thu, 11 Dec 2014 19:48:03

Eternal God, Jesus, Love
My love, there was a young man
In full uniform, walking in a shining
Light, leaving footprints in freshly
Fallen snow – angels above singing peace

In the night – so cold- frozen darkness
If a shot was fired – the garden
Would have fractured into lost pieces
His rifle mad him King of the World
The only noise – crunching of snow
Beneath the boots

My love – how far away – the announcing
Star – how far away that silent night
Love is fading – angels no longer sing
No one waits for the star – gone
What is left for the young man
Daring not to fire a shot – explosion heard

The heavens weep tears of snowflakes
Son to learn all about war
Soon to learn all about dying
There was plenty of time – Just seventeen
He left early – leaving echoes of crunching snow
Beneath his boots – it was time
To learn all about war and dying

Prayer Book Page 101

Thu, 18 Dec 2014 14:01:05

Eternal God, Jesus, Love
My Love, in the ways of wisdom
Spirit speaks – providing an offering
In great joy – praying please
Accept all that I am – never again
To be me – no longer obligated to self
In this – a new beginning
Consumed in your glory

Freedom alive – in you – no need
To feel obligated to self
Or the nothingness of senseless being
Fulfillment in you – consumed in your love
Now ending – self fading in you
In you my love I have placed who I am
No more demands of self
You are the only reason, my love   to exist

My love – please take all that is me
Into your Godliness – allow no more
Imperfections of me
Let the last moment be born in you
To know only you – eternally – my love
In your veins Holy God to live
Eternal – no longer me
Only as you – the greatest joy

Prayer Book Page 102

Tue, 30 Dec 2014 20:32:46

Eternal God, Jesus, Love
My love, time to pause
To recommend to your sacred heart
Asking for your magnificent love
To reach a special spirit
One who gives joy – from the heart

May your name be spoken
On her behalf – drawing special graces
Of your love – embracing her
For the gift of kindness

Each moment of kindness is never
Forgotten, but lives forever
IN the hearts of angels singing praise

In times of tears and heavy emotions
Kindness softens the hurt and pain
Lifting wounded spirit above the cry

Reach in your love this gentle soul
Giving of self – to share with love
Years of passing – time to come
She remains remembered – her kindness lives forever

(Thank you Jessica)

Prayer Book Page 103

Sat, 10 Jan 2015 11:09:14

Eternal God, Jesus, Love
My love, spirit has struggled
To find a gift for you - in thanksgiving
For the wonderful graces you give
Answering our prayers – through every day

In the ways of an imperfect garden
Only love and gratitude can serve
Still the longing cannot be ended
To hold you – one time – in your splendor
Look into your eyes – giving to spirit
The greatest joy – embracing the eternal

Only you can give true comfort
Peace in a turbulent garden
Spirit is fearful you will turn away
Abandoning the garden to the slavery of darkness

Nothing else matters beyond you
No past – no future – only eternal love
Oneness with you – fulfills all desire
In your resurrection – becoming ever lasting

No joy is greater than the joy of you
Filling every heart with your magnificent
Love offered from the cross
Given freely from the depths of divinity

Prayer Book Page 104

Fri, 16 Jan 2015 21:25:09

Eternal God, Jesus, Love
My love – it happed this way
The man – wore a long brown robe
And hood – with a knotted white rope
At his side – entangled with a rosary

Curiosity led to him – do not ask who
I am – or where I come from – his voice firm
My silence agreed – sitting quiet to listen
I come here every day – to be with
The son of God – to hold him – this man
Suffering – who is God
In him I pray for the garden
Speedily on its way to hell

Keeling and holding the cross
Great sorrow and suffering gripped the man
In the brown robe – never moving away
Reaching for him – my hands were depleted
Upward allowing me to have moments
Sharing his efforts to save mankind

He repeated – too many serve the darkness
Their pleasure seeking turns them away from
The heavenly kingdom and eternal life
My love – it does appear you have shed your blood
In vain – so many have rejected you
Choosing evil and eternal death
The man in the robe left mysteriously – calling out loudly – pray

Prayer Book Page 105

Wed, 21 Jan 2015 22:25:59

Eternal God, Jesus, Love
My Love – This day – Holy One
Pleading for your divine mercy
For all the sick and suffering in the garden

Grant – Holy One your magnificent healing love
Embrace the sick and suffering – in their illness
They cry out to you though engulfed in pain
Waiting in hope for your arrival – bringing healing

Holy One – grant your compassion to the children
Unable to understand – how their young bodies
Are filled with such grief and suffering
Have mercy on them – turn their sorrow to joy
Remove the heavy crosses they have to carry

Holy One – accept our own suffering on behalf of the sick
End their sadness – in your own heart
There is no comfort greater than your love
Holy One – grant the grace of life
To this prayer

Prayer Book Page 106

Sat, 31 Jan 2015 18:28:59

Eternal God, Jesus, Love
My Love – Holy One – spirit
Is buoyed this morning
Prayers bring warmth of your love
Like sunshine – throughout the heavens

Please Holy One grant to all
Reaching for you – grace of peace
Grant our prayers for a
Joyful life – in the way of you

Holy One – praying for the
Lonely and abandoned – embrace
Them in your divine love
Let them feel the closeness of you

My Love – Savior – there is suffering
For your magnificent love on the cross
Reaching beyond the daily hours
In each moment – praying for the forgiveness of sin

Holy One – my love – do not pass
So many in need – seeking you
Call to holiness every heart – to join
You – mercy and love everlasting
In this prayer – they live in you

Prayer Book Page 107

Sun, 08 Feb 2015 19:22:58

Eternal God, Jesus, Love
My love, long ago it was heard
This world is passing away
With meaning still strong
Holy One – what prayer can be offered
To bring lasting peace to our garden
That it not pass away in evil destruction

Spirit prays for your divine mercy
Holy One – please reach and embrace every heart
Wandering in the loneliness of separation
From you – living without hope
Enflame them in your love – save your children

Spirit prays for the peace – only you can give
Peace that ends separation and loneliness
Spirit prays for the sick and the dying
Silence the pain and sorrow
Let the light of your love be seen
Loving and healing – lifting all
Into your kingdom – to the joy of eternal life

My love – prayer can take away the darkness
Holy One – spirit yearns for the holiness
Of the union in you – let the angels sing of
Your embrace – prayer has been granted
Divine Love – your love – is supreme

Prayer Book Page 108

Sun, 22 Feb 2015 20:40:32

Eternal God, Jesus, Love

My Love, spirit dwells in a house of mystery

Pressing to understand your voice

Causing things to be – the truth of you

Holy One – prayer seeks to understand

You becoming one with man – the

Creator one with the created

Your voice – tells – the power of the

Most High will overshadow you – woman

Full of grace – before he emerges

His name is – Jesus

Birth by your voice of the – God-man

Lives to endure great and terrible suffering

Salvation found in magnificent love

When "it is finished" prayer seeks

To reach that moment wherein evil is defeated

Holy One – In three days you rebuild the temple

Prayer seeks to enter the promise of

Resurrection – eternal

This prayer seeks the holiest and greatest

Of all mysteries – the living Eucharist

Divine love embracing each soul

In eternal communion – from the cross

Of salvation to the completion of the

Final hour- passing into new life – in you

Prayer Book Page 110

Wed, 25 Feb 2015 22:35:16

Eternal God, Jesus, Love
My love, a terrible war is engulfing
The garden – sons of darkness slaughter
For the will of the gre at liar – furious
In anger – To satisfy the first criminal
Seeking to destroy our garden and
Replace it with an evil kingdom
Turning the light and love of you
Into hate and suffocating darkness
Holy One, The evil children
Seek to destroy the Cross of Salvation
And you my love, to lift another
As the Son of God
My Love, call your faithful to
Fill the churches – to pray intensely
For the defeat of the rampant evil
That serves only death and destruction
Enlighten your children – Holy One
Let Faith burn in every believing
Heart – destroy the rebellion – seeking
To destroy the Cross of Salvation
Fill your churches with prayer
To end the conflagration – rebellion
In service to the liar – filling darkness
With death and destruction
My Love, please send your Holy Angel
To defeat this evil war, though we
Die in battle – we know in the end – you
Eternal God – will be victorious

Prayer Book Page 111

Fri, 13 Mar 2015 20:07:29

Eternal God, Jesus, Love
My Love – This prayer pleads
Your mercy be upon all the
Sick and suffering in the garden

Holy One – so much weeping
Our garden cannot contain so many
Tears – drowning so many flowers
Let your mercy embrace them
Lift their spirit to the joy of you

This prayer pleads to understand
The way of agony breaking life
Supremely useless, spirit feels
Unable to touch the pain – and silence it

My love – hold in your sacred heart
The suffering of so many in the garden
Gather their tears
Live in them – giving new life
In your self – healing them

Holy One – lift each spirit in pain
Into pure freedom – with compassion
In eternal union with you

Prayer Book Page 112

Thu, 19 Mar 2015 20:03:31

Eternal God, Jesus, Love
My love, great wandering
Has taken hold in the garden
Endless searching - for a place of calm
To rest for brief moments
In peace – let the quiet
Consume – all fear and trembling

Holy One – our days seek
The miracle of your love – to save
Our garden
End the wandering in darkness
Only the miracle of your love
Can give healing to our garden

Holy One – difficult is the way
To understanding how darkness
Is so overwhelming – punishing
Tender hearts – leading them to wander
Without hope – longing only for a
Small place to rest – away from the
Shattering suffering inflicted by evil
Please my love extend your heart
Grant once again peace in the garden
Good Shepard – please……

Prayer Book Page 113

Sat, 28 Mar 2015 19:27:11

Eternal God, Jesus, Love
My love, this day I am led
To ask – why are churches so empty
Someone has to make the call
Go to God's house and pray
Before evil destroys the house and garden

Is there too much luxury
Suffocating faith and desire
For you my love – too much indulgence
In clamorous things – causing the faithful
To love those of position – alleged humitly
And false holiness – reject you –
The true holiness

My love, where are your callers of faith
The one in the dark suits and white
Collars – where are they to brighten
The days and nights – leading in prayer

Holy One – such darkness – difficult
To understand – why so many have
Turned away from you - embracing emptiness
Why my love are the churches lonely places
So many hearts turning cold
Shepherds failing
As the children of the garden
Slip into hell

Prayer Book Page 114

Wed, 01 Apr 2015 20:32:03

Eternal God, Jesus, Love
My love, for such a long time
Wanting to speak of something very special
The magnificent joy of you

How is it possible to live without
The great happiness of your love
Every prayer brings you near – very near
Your love fills the heart with such joy
There is an overflowing joy – warming
And comforting in great happiness

My love, the joy of you is given
Life to every prayer – in the peace
Of you – sharing angelic singing praising you
One day Holy One – you will grant the
Greatest joy – holding you – within
For now to be – in the Eucharist

My joy, my love, my peace – my life
Can only be in and with you
This prayer is for all the children in the garden
To reach for you and know your love
And the great joy you offer
Your love – Holy One – is the purest joy

Prayer Book Page 115

Eternal God, Jesus, Love
My Love, it does appear, your chosen
City is in grave danger –
Jerusalem – is in great peril

Notice in that name my love
Jerusalem carries another
Name – see Jerusalem – awesome
You declared the city your own
Did you see USA the same time

Has Judas returned – waiting
To inflict his second horrific kiss
Of betrayal – hoping destruction of the city
Holding all of US away in fear

Who will come to stop the Judas kiss
Who will come and defeat the traitor
Servant of the liar – rest in hell

Judas waits in darkness – his betrayal
Set to destroy the Holy City
The traitor will also betray His own
If not stopped – gone is the Holy City
And USA with it – will the traitor succeed

Prayer Book Page 116

Sun, 19 Apr 2015 21:58:27

Eternal God, Jesus, Love,
My love, to suffer for your
Magnificent love on the cross
There is no greater desire
To be one with you – Holy One
There is no greater reward

Let the love in every heart reaching for you
Live on through the final hour
To live in you forever
A precious gift from each life

My love, surely you understand
How difficult each day becomes
When we try to be like you
And carry over crosses behind you
Your blood very often blocks our way
We fall many times

Holy one, there is only one question
How many times will you forgive us
Seeing how foolish and weak we are
How long will your mercy remain
How long will you help us to get up
And keep going
Until we stand in front of you
To lean on your magnificent love

Prayer Book Page 117

Sat, 25 Apr 2015 22:13:55

Eternal God, Jesus, Love
My love, surely it was a dream
The Lady in White woke me in spirit
Her stunning beauty and glory
Lifted me without touching

Going beside her she seemed to float
Together we entered a great light
That gave me life – God's own light

"Would you like to meet my Son?" she asked
"Oh, yes." I replied quickly. "I will
Ask him to let me stay with you,
Never to go back." There was never
Any notice of my own voice – how
Was I thinking – how was I existing

Sweet perfume blessed me
Touching and lifting my spirit – lovely comfort
A great crowd unseen gathered around us
Praising the glorious Lady in White
She smiled – peace reigned

Moving to leave the heavenly place
Still buoyed in spirit
The Lady in White – left me
In her glory, quietly fading into heavenly light

Prayer Book Page 118

Sat, 02 May 2015 13:22:14

Eternal God, Jesus, Love
My love, many times I wonder
If today mankind will hear
Loudly in the heavens
"Enough is enough" the garden fell into darkness

Nothing on the earth moved
No wind – no rain – nothing – no sounds
Only darkness – where is mankind?
Peace on earth at last

Through pain and suffering
Resurrection did not end anger
Now even the grass is dying
No voices call out for mercy for the garden

Wait! There is a tiny spec of light
Far off – coming so fast to explode in the darkness
The Lady in White is pleading - holding
The most magnificent one – Her Son

One more chance, my son – give
Them one more chance – Her tears in a flood
The magnificent one spoke – you
Test my heat My Love – this time
I will grant your prayer – there was light
The garden lived again

Prayer Book Page 119

Mon, 11 May 2015 23:10:21

Eternal God, Jesus, Love
My Love, the path to your cross
Every day is not easy – each step – pain
Standing there for hours – desire burning
Unable to hold you – spirit weeps

Trying to understand your pain
And suffering – unable to share
Your agony – separation becomes
Unbearable – comfort remains unknown

Only those who truly love you
Can understand the extent of
Spiritual loneliness gripping the soul
In that place where only you can live

Holy One, there is only trembling
Moving away from your cross
There is no freedom from pain filled moments
No beginning – no end – each embrace eternal

My love – spirit will walk again
To your cross – accepting anew
Each pain of your agony – in hope
To live in your everlasting love
In your eternal life – spirit will
Embrace you – in the last
Walk to your cross

Prayer Book Page 120

Thu, 21 May 2015 09:29:20

Eternal God, Jesus, Love
My Love, this prayer is offered
With great sadness and hope
For all who have turned away
Leaving you alone on the cross

Forgive them Holy One – for abandoning
The wounds of salvation – wounds
Of magnificent love – call them to return
To hold your love within themselves

If only one soul will return
Great joy will rise in heaven
The garden will sing with the angels
Each wound will know and give glory

Through many days and nights
In the great fragrance of your love
Quiet in the garden will call many souls

To reach for you – Holy One
True friend – spirit is there
Seeking to join you and share
The suffering of your cross – one heart
Holding your love – every wound
Your magnificent love – eternal

Prayer Book Page 121

Sun, 07 Jun 2015 20:54:43

Eternal God, Jesus, Love
My Love, fill the heavens
With prayers of love
For all who are sick
In the fragrance of your healing love

Gather the tears of the sick
Those who suffer through endless hours
Send forth your Holy Spirit
Hold them in your divine compassion

Holy One, give yourself to so many
Sick, dispel all fear and despair
In your healing love end the darkness
Of pain and suffering they bear

You, Holy One, are the hope
Carried in their silence
Let not abandonment to pain and suffering
Carry them through the hours

Look upon all the sick in the garden
Your brothers and sisters long for healing
So many, my love, need you, your love
Touch them in your divinity
Lift them to peace and serenity
Lift them in your healing love

Prayer Book Page 123

Thu, 30 Jul 2015 14:25:01

Eternal God, Jesus, Love
My love, eve is rampant
Flooding the garden – blood
Of the innocent - the only way now
Only prayer – reaching for hope

The garden you brought forth
Through your word, "It is good"
Now the garden – a mere slaughter house
The anger of hell – drawing blood
Even babies – have no love to save them

This prayer, Holy One – begging you
To come back – fill the garden with your love
End the evil – pain and suffering
Embrace the blood of innocents

Welcome into your kingdom
All destroyed in the flesh – hands of evil
Be their living comfort - as they live in you
Devour the evil ones – let their hate - end in the fires of hell

Holy One, please come back
End the time from when you were lifted up fully crucified
To this very moment – the vein of evil
Let the joy of you Jesus – renew every heart
In peace, your eternal love
End the days of evil – forever – by your word

Prayer Book Page 124

Fri, 10 Jul 2015 19:45:08

Eternal God, Jesus, Love
My love, Glory of my heart
Fearing the day - living without you
This prayer pleads for your love
To hold you and let me fade into divinity

Holy One, why the distance between
Life and love, conclusions never reached
Mental wanderings confusing the soul
All that you are beyond mortal grasp

The meaning of emptiness found
When each soul weeps for your love
Held in darkness waiting for the
Moment for life giving love - eternal

Possibilities no longer existing
One direction the lone way to go
Only to you, Holy One - hope lives
Eternal God, Jesus, love - free

Bonds of love - unrestrained - glorious
Majesty embracing - light to the soul
Unending love - filling veins - eternal life
In God alone - living - loving - holding
Impossible to find - separation

Prayer Book Page 125

Sun, 28 Jun 2015 22:11:32

Eternal God, Jesus, Love
My love, in the midst of pain
And suffering – speaking your name
Your spirit blossoms in my soul

Holy One, the way is never clear
Distance between peace and pain
Is not spoken seriously
Leaving a yearning for respite

My love, all need help and hope
With the approach of day ending
Each moment waits for your embrace
Fill the spirit in divine mercy

In the silence, my love, the pain
Is not felt, no attention given
Only your love is embracing
Your magnificent love on the cross

Reaching to the very depth of our being
Tracing more than outlines of our souls
The image and likeness of you
Renders glory in the softness of you.

Prayer Book Page 126

Thu, 30 Jul 2015 14:36:01

Eternal God, Jesus, Love
My love, weeping fills our garden
So much suffering – no escape
Touching all, beyond understanding
Sorrow reaches for intervention
Often spreading across the garden – cold silence

Holy One, imbedded mystery
Goes on – not much revelation
Spirit touched – nothing given
Beyond the hours – emptiness
Only you my love – only you are real

Nothing – Takes over everything
Yet faith continues – believing in truth
Found in the little white host – eternal life
Add nothing – give nothing – only love

Holy One, a large empty cross
Stands lonely in the church
Urgent to tear it down, leave it – was spoken
Lest his blood flow every where

Fill every heart – sustaining love
Extend us beyond now into your arms
In grace hold us in your
Magnificent love on the cross

Prayer Book Page 127

Thu, 06 Aug 2015 10:59:42

Eternal God, Jesus, Love
My Love, a beautiful light stands
In the center of the garden
Few go to it, for most it has no meaning
Not even the cross within
Some find your peace – Holy One
That which the world cannot give
Yet, offered freely to all

Not easy to understand – why
So few reach into the light – the cross
Preferring instead the false peace
Of the world – blinding the spirit
Holding the heart in lies

My love, let the truth of your peace
Dispel lies, devour despair and darkness

This prayer, eternal one – claim your peace
Your grace and love for every soul
That which flows in the light
For all, your peace – love – truth

My love, from the light let your peace
Fill every heart, quiet the raging
Storms within – to live each day
In your peace – this the world
Cannot give

Prayer Book Page 128

Mon, 10 Aug 2015 12:03:01

Eternal God, Jesus, Love
My love, thinking in the spirit
How long will it be – for you to allow
Me to hold on to you – for the final
Act of purification – living the cross with you

The path ahead is perilous
Rocks and stones twist the feet
Many still coated with blood
Show the way to the place called the skull

Holy One Let me hold on to you
Lest I fall and fail the magnificent love
Glowing in your eyes – and soon will begin
Flowing from your pierced heart

Separation from you my love
Is life without hope – useless
Let me hold on to you Holy One
If I fail your love – heaven will disappear

Holy One, I must hold on to you
Even to raising of you pierced on the cross
For sure I can't let go as I dread
The loss of heaven
Most of all I dread the loss of your love

Prayer Book Page 129

Sun, 23 Aug 2015 10:02:55

Eternal God, Jesus, Love
My Love, the Lady in white returned
After such a long time – great joy
Dream or vision – remains unknown
Her comforting smile – all embracing
Held time still- endless joy

Voice soft and sweet
With concern – not enough children
Of the garden are praying – few are taking
His love given freely in sacrifice
No tears this time – yet known to be
There is great sorrow coming

Her light faded – leaving fragrance
Truth is given – tell everyone reach – for his love
Children of the garden pray as never before
Reach for eternal love – peace

Let your prayers suffocate the evil
That lures once pure hearts into the
Darkness – destroying them
There is wonder and joy to hold
Simply reach for it – fill your lives
With His happiness – pray away – the
Darkness – that gives only fear and destruction
Let your prayers embrace the cross
Reach for Him for true freedom

Prayer Book Page 130

Tue, 01 Sep 2015 10:22:23

Eternal God, Jesus, Love
My love, spirit weeps – children
Of the garden – suffering – without hope
Evil triumphant – laughs at their agony

Angels singing bring light for the garden
Holding back violent threats
Prepared by the darkness – pending
Pain and suffering

My love – the garden is afflicted
Upheaval – children wandering – homeless
Prayers reaching for you – my love
Return – let them breathe the fragrance of hope

Holy One – stand at the gates of the garden
Let your breath – cause peace – to the children
Abandoned – suffering through endless hours
Of fear – loneliness – hunger

Holy One – babies of the garden
Call out to you – end their tears – grant mercy
End the evil – hold them in your love
Free them from explosions of hat
In the home of your heart
Let the joy of you – be their peace - forever

Prayer Book Page 131

Fri, 04 Sep 2015 08:50:01

Eternal God, Jesus, Love
My love, spirit turns to sing
Love song to you
Carried quietly – such a long time

For sure angels have been heard
Singing the same love song
My love, words flow – alive in flight
Finding your heart – forever

Moments begin and end – in softness
The song of love is fulfilled
Sweetly embracing – your heart
Eternity – suspended with each touch

Spirit trembles as you come near
Singing words so sublime
My love, my love divine
Spirit lives – you are mine

Holy One – you sing a sweetened song
Memories are stirred – to live a new
Love is all that can be
The splendor of you – holding me

Prayer Book Page 132

Tue, 22 Sep 2015 15:09:33

Eternal God, Jesus, Love
My Love, this prayer is offered
For all of the weary children of the
Garden – Holding everything which is nothing
Living each moment without connection

Holy One – see especially those so young
Seemingly wandering through aimless hours
Searching for meaningless – empty things
My Love – be there for them – fill their hearts
With your love – and be their peace

So difficult to be reaching every day
And touch nothing – children of the garden
Need truth – of you – in your light hold them

Let them find you – embrace – be all that is
Real for them – end the useless searching
The world cannot give peace to a restless heart
Call to yourself all of the wandering
In your love – guide and teach – Holy One
Lead them in – your way

Prayer Book Page 133

Sat, 26 Sep 2015 21:39:49

Eternal God, Jesus, Love
My love, this prayer pleads
Open your sacred heart to all
In the garden – grant to them
The highest and greatest joy
Your magnificent love on the cross

Mend every heart – Holy One
Injured through the tragedy of sin
The Joy of you healing all who reach for you
Joy that ends – pain and suffering

Let everyone in the garden know
You are the only way of salvation
Show them the joy of your light
Hold all in the purity of your spirit

My Love, this prayer pleads for you
Not to leave in loneliness – your children
Call them to your words of eternal life
Promises of peace – love - hope
The joy of you - unending

Prayer Book Page 134

Wed, 07 Oct 2015 14:14:06

Eternal God, Jesus, Love
My Love, there is a beggar on the road
With tears in his eyes – unable to understand
Why so many in the garden
Have emptied themselves and thrown away their faith

Reaching for all the worldly treasures
Your children squander the hours
On foolish and empty things
The beggar pleads for you Holy One
To restore your children before they are lost

How can it be – my love – so few
Return to the church to receive you in the Eucharist
When – once they believed so completely – and loved
Receiving you – your joy and peace

The beggar reaches for you
Weeps for them – where are the children, he asks
Once loving you – now abandoning your love
The beggar weeps for all in the garden
So close to being lost – in eternal emptiness

Call them back – Holy One – back to you
Give them your love – eternal
Let them know – you wait
With love – the beggar weeps – in prayer
Embrace the children of the garden – Holy One

Prayer Book Page 135

Wed, 14 Oct 2015 14:04:22

Eternal God, Jesus, Love
My Love – distance – here to you
Heavy and difficult – once
Discovered and understood

The most difficult mystery – Holy One
Searching through all that can be found
Is you – My Love – seekers in the garden
Want to know – the way of the cross
How did you do it – pain and suffering

Holy One – so much space – filled with anger
Prayers needed – send holy angels to sing
Let all in the garden join them
Sharing in the joy of being with you

There is one approaching – before your cross
In front of you trembling – feeling
Cast in pain – he waits the agony
In his arms – holding you

Love is overwhelming – he is – become like you
Holding you – never to let go
Two hearts beating as one – love is joined
Now and forever – living in every wound

Prayer Book Page 136

Wed, 14 Oct 2015 14:09:43

Eternal God, Jesus, Love
My love, your children in the garden
Cry out for the embrace of the
Joy of you – the embrace of your glory

Only the holy one can give the joy
Of everlasting hope – peace – love
Your children cry out a great need
The joy of you – to live in your glory

One glimpse – Holy One – seeing
In the spirit your magnificence
Throughout the kingdom – your place
At the right hand of the father

My love, the garden is wounded
Please, Holy One embrace your children
Hold them in your light
Greeting them in the grace of your mercy

Yes, Holy One – they are your children
Suffering because you are so far away
Call them, let them hear your voice
Give them all the magnificent joy of you
Please, Holy One remember those
Who love you – so completely
Let their longing embrace you
To be joy for you

Prayer Book Page 137

Fri, 23 Oct 2015 12:43:30

Eternal God, Jesus, Love
My love, spirit remembers
From so far away a tiny spec
Light came – eyes of the soul opened
Suspended between life and death
Eternal life – eternal death
No light – no life – simple
A distant place – eternal he lived

The explosion – light all around
Above him – below – in him
Giving him life – if taken away
He would slip into darkness
And surely die – love blessed spirit
Life continued

Holy One – spirit waits the light
Longing – to know you again
Such glory seen – all else – nothing

My love – please hold close – your children
In the garden – reaching for you
Receive their prayers – of love
Calling in the midst of sorrow and suffering
Holding you on the cross – in their own
Eternal love

Bless the garden in your light
Protect all who are there
Loving you – let your light
Ignite their souls with life
Embrace all in your love
Send the eternal spec of light
Saturating them with eternal life

Prayer Book Page 139

Tue, 10 Nov 2015 16:12:57

Eternal God, Jesus, Love
My Love, Spirit waits in terrible loneliness
To hold you, Holy One, in one
Magnificent embrace – love eternal

So many in the garden
Seek union with you – Holy One
To know fully – the comfort
That only you can give

Who is it walking the path
Every day to you on the cross – Holy One
Reaching for you – suffering
Asking only for the warmth of your love

Who is it walking the path
Reaching for you – suffering – knowing
You alone offer to all in the garden
Sweetest - gentlest – loving peace

The one who walks to you – seeks
To share the wounds – the pain – the cross
Knowing the splendor of your love
In union – oneness - forever

Prayer Book Page 140

Wed, 02 Dec 2015 14:22:02

Eternal God, Jesus, love
My love – the situation in the garden
Has reached a point of desperation
The slaughter has worsened

Holy One – please help to end the battle
Against the sons of Satan possessed by
Demons from the darkest depths of hell
Gorging themselves on blood of innocents

Gather out prayers quickly – my love
Before the evil ones desecrate them
Along with our fallen loved ones
Here and in faraway cities

Holy One – embrace the fallen
Slain by the sons of Satan
Violating all that is sacred and holy

Grant the grace needed to face
The evil that waits to strike
Filling more graves with their evil
The grace Holy One to stand without fear
Stout of heart – firm in faith
To triumph over Satan's legions
We will sing with the angels
Sons and daughters free
Marching on forever for the joy of victory

Prayer Book Page 142

Fri, 18 Dec 2015 22:57:53

Eternal God, Jesus, Love
My Love, passing years
Reveal, dear Holy One
You are the purest love

Please come back Holy One
End the pain and suffering
On your children in the garden
Evil has launched the final struggle

My Love, this prayer is offered
On behalf of all in the garden
Who have remained loyal to you
and who have not abandoned you
Leaving you alone in agony on the cross

So many have chosen emptiness
And darkness for their souls
Throwing away their faith

In your compassion Holy One
Show them your magnificent love
Call them back - help them to know
You still love them
Even in their abandonment of you

Prayer Book Page 143

Eternal God, Jesus, Love
My Love, this prayer is offered
Into your divinity for all of
Your seriously ill children in the garden
Many are preparing to leave
And in their suffering have no faith
To help them or guide them
Having, so long ago, forgotten your name

My Love, please do not discount their suffering
Their pain, surely in harsh times they prayed
Sometimes when suffering is so harsh
We are unable to pray or speak your name

This prayer is offered in their name
That you, my Love, will hear my voice
On their lips and call them
Through the darkness to your love – life

Holy One, how is it so many
Can pass through life – and at the end
Find only darkness and emptiness
Having forgotten your name
And your magnificent love on the cross
You are there – waiting for them

Prayer Book Page 144

Mon, 11 Jan 2016 16:09:38

Eternal God, Jesus, Love
My Love, the garden has fallen
Into disarray – your children are
In the grip of terrible conflict
The great stream of life is being
Filtered – with ominous signs
Depleting the wonderful grace of – hope
Many of your children live with
Barren hearts – without hope

This very moment – strange songs
Are being sung – escape into false
Doctrines overwhelmingly capture
Your children – leaving them without hope
Unable to live in the peace you offer
Hope – stolen by fear leaves them empty

Holy one – please come back
Fill each heart with your magnificent love
Restore their faith – giving them renewed
Grace of hope – defeat their fears
In your love – guide them away from
The ominous signs in the garden
Call all of your children to the live again in the hope
You offer – peace found only in you
The joy of you

Prayer Book Page 145

Eternal God, Jesus, Love
My Love, this prayer is offered
For all in the garden who long
For you, faithfully, everyday
To look into your eyes – receive
Your magnificent forgiving love
Never ending love – Holy One

Their longing for you – takes them
Every day to your cross – taking into
Themselves every wound – every pain
Holding secure your magnificent love

Only in standing before you – seeing crucifying
The truth of your love for them
Are they allowing themselves to enter
The way of life – salvation – hope alive

The only grace they seek – the goodness
Of you – holding on to you – sharing
The total gift of you – life is fulfilled
Seeking nothing more but you – Holy one

Give them all that you are – living in you
Let them see you – as the call for you
They are the prayer reaching you Holy One
Away from you there is nothing – in love
With you – they are entering - complete

Prayer Book Page 146

Thu, 11 Feb 2016 16:02:10

Eternal God, Jesus, Love
My Love, time to pray – to embrace you
For so many in the garden
Suffering in terrible ways
If their suffering – their pain
Does not carry them into your
Hear – Holy One – it means nothing
And has no purpose

There are time when the pain
Is so severe – you holy name
Cannot pass their lips
The call is for death to end all
Hope does not live in pain
Yet they keep a candle burning for your love

So many find only hard sleep in suffering
Never knowing if your touch held them
Now – in prayer – we speak for them
Your mercy – compassion – healing love
Comfort them – free them – live in them

Without you Holy One – suffering is meaningless
Your light and love provides the way
To peace – and comfort – desire to
Live within you – in your love
Who knows pain and suffering more than you
Bless all who suffer this day
Your heart, Holy One will remain broken until all of your children are healed

Prayer Book Page 147

Thu, 18 Feb 2016 22:59:39

Eternal God, Jesus, Love
My Love, this prayer of thanksgiving offered
To you, Holy One – for so many gifts
From your heart – first – the gift of faith

Far above so many gifts – Holy One
Containing all that you are
Your resurrection – and ours

Through your gift of prayer
We can send you – your healing love
To all who hurt and who are wounded
Anywhere and everywhere in the garden

Thank you, Holy One for the gift
Of the Holy Eucharist – received in truth
Thank you for the gift of you

Thank you my life – for so many gifts
Your love embracing – giving life
Fill every heart with the joy of you
Forgiving – sins – leading all to eternal life

Thank you, Holy One – for the Lady in White
Unsurpassed purity – captured her words in history
"Let it be done." Forever an extraordinary gift
The Lady in White – leading everyone to you
Holy One, on the cross – share your magnificent love

Prayer Book Page 148

Eternal God, Jesus, Love
My Love, one man was praying
In the midst of my pain and suffering
Holy One I speak your name
In these moments peace embraces – spirit

Another man prayed somber – Holy One
Please, my Love, do not allow
The darkness of the demons
Destroy my love for you
It cannot destroy your love for me

A soft voice was heard in holy love
Saying – I will carry my pain and suffering
Into my last hour – with one request
Through each moment of suffering – my love
Let me hold onto you – lest my desire
Weaken causing me to fail
And not obtain – you magnificent love on the cross

Holy angels fill the heavens above the garden
Praising eternal goodness in sweet music
Divine love is eternal – for all who reach for it
Voices rise from the garden – praying
You Holy One – give you love – fill them
Let their spirits glow in you

Prayer Book Page 149

Tue, 08 Mar 2016 16:14:29

Eternal God, Jesus Love
My Love, so many years have passed
Many filled with joy and laughter
Now, Holy One, it is time to ask
For a very special grace in the words
Of this prayer

Holy One, this prayer reaching to you
For that special grace that will call me
To be your servant – not at some distance
From you but being alive in your
Divinity – one with you as you are one
With the Father – dissolved in your holy divinity
No longer me – but being you

How is it my love, this longing never
Before became the fruit of my life
Please let it be – for whatever time is left
To be your servant into my final hours
Born forever – my love   your servant
Living in you – eternal truth

Please Holy One, let this prayer
Carry the names of all who love you
Embracing your sacred heart – receiving your precious love
In the light bursting from your
Magnificent Divinity

Prayer Book Page 150

Thu, 17 Mar 2016 13:16:44

Eternal God, Jesus, Love
My love, this prayer is to
Embrace your sacred heart
And plead for you Holy One
For all of your brothers and sisters
Who love you unto death -
Knowing your magnificent love forever
On the cross

Surely, Holy One, you know
Their names – their hearts
Filled with love for you –
Seeking to share your suffering
Each moment of inflicted pain
Seeking to understand the
Extent of your love for them

Holy One you know their names
Ready for any cross – even to death
To be with you – into eternity
Their love for you rising to mingle
And dissolve in your love for them
Holy One, remember their – names
Remember their – love living in you

Prayer Book Page 151

Tue, 22 Mar 2016 16:08:02

Eternal God, Jesus, Love
My love, the valleys across the garden
are filling with wandering souls
unable to find rest or peace simply
carrying their pain and suffering

Holy One, the roses are fading
saturated in the tears of your children
their voices rise through endless quiet nights
Prayers once sung suffocated in the cold
Darkness of empty stars - there is no love

Holy one, they wait for you to weep with them
to embrace their sorrow - point to each one
declare they are your own - there will be an accounting

My love, more come every day - filling
the valleys - soon no space will be available
shifting their feet everyday - wandering on
meeting new hours with tears - their souls
filled with exhaustion - once beautiful smiles
rusting away - waiting for you Holy One
Evil has feasted so long on hearts once
filled with hope - calling for your
compassion - Holy One live tomorrow
My love they will be gone - new shifting
will replace them- suffering will go on

Prayer Book Page 152

Eternal God, Jesus, Love
My Love, this prayer is calling for the
Power and glory of your holy name
To free your children from the rampant
And raging evil in the garden

My Love send the power and glory
Of your holy name – to fill the hearts
Of those who love you – free them from fear
In the grace of your peace, renew
Hope in them – in the fragrance of your love

Let the power and glory of your holy name
Silence forever all evil seeking to
Captivate your children – to destroy their
Hope – love – peace – your offer

Holy one – fill the garden with joy and singing
Love found only in your embrace – that lasts
Forever – in the power and glory of your
Holy name – forever – they seek to live

My Love – into the power and glory of your holy name
Your children flee from evil – leaving behind
Pain and suffering – knowing they can live only in you
Forever beyond the touches of evil
The power and glory of your holy name
They know, leads them to eternal life

Prayer Book Page 153

Fri, 08 Apr 2016 15:49:13

Eternal God, Jesus, Love
My Love, a great cry is
Rising from the garden
Not in rebellion, Holy One
But from divine intervention – Help

So many are unable to rise each day
And receive you in Eucharist, Holy One
There is a great need of divine help
You are needed Holy One to fill each heart
With the bread of life – until then
Crying in the garden will continue

Why my love do we hide you
In a little box - take you at various times
Then return you into the darkness
Of the little box – the tabernacle

Those who cannot rise – cry to
Take you into themselves – they know
And believe you live in the Eucharist
They wait for you to find them
There is no doubt they know
Eternal life – receiving you in the Eucharist

Pronyer Book Page 154

Thu, 14 Apr 2016 09:01:14

Eternal God, Jesus, Love
My Love, angels with flaming swords
Have been seen in various parts
Of the garden piercing spirits
Who have chosen evil to live by

What is happening to your children
So shallow – empty – void of a future
Empty shells far away from the time
When you saw them as being good in so many ways

Love is dying in the garden – why
You are being blamed – Holy One
Errors continue in the choices they make
Hatred runs rampant
And still you love them

Hope is the mead of evil
A great darkness fills souls – lost
From the light – come back Holy One
Fill the garden with light – your light
Your love – call them to walk with you
To live in you – the joy of you
They cry for you – call them Holy One
Save them from the pain and suffering
They will surely face – losing you
Holy One – as they lose eternal life

Prayer Book Page 155

Tue, 19 Apr 2016 08:44:23

Eternal God, Jesus, Love
My Love, how long, Holy One
Has spirit walked in the pathways
Of the garden hoping to see you
Hear your voice – thank you
For your magnificent love
On the cross

Remember the time
Holy One – The tiny spec of light
Racing through infinity – exploding
All around especially within
Opening spirits eyes – to the
Life giving light

If the pathways of the garden
Should end – thank you Holy One
For that tiny spec of light giving life
Surely spirit waits for the light to come again
To leave the garden and be
With you Holy One forever
In that tiny spec of light that
Exploded all around – especially within
Giving life to spirit who learned
No light – no life

Prayer Book Page 156

Thu, 28 Apr 2016 15:11:33

Eternal God, Jesus, Love
My Love, this prayer is for you alone
Direct to your sacred heart – Holy One
Please come to be with your family
In the garden – so many requests waiting

Please Holy One, Grant one day
Of peace – your peace - to be felt
Through your very presence – one day
In your embrace – without fear of
Raging evil – one day

Grant one day – Holy One – free of pain
And suffering – free every heart to live
In the comfort of your love – one day
Grant one day – Holy One – filled with grace
Let all in the garden look into your eyes
With their tears – tell you how much
They love you – seeking to share your terrible
Suffering on the cross – one day – one with you

One day – Holy One – for all in the garden
The pure joy of your – let their joy
Be offering to all they meet
One day – Holy One – show your light
Throughout the heavens – for all to see
Just one day my love – your children
Can know how good – life can be

One day – Holy One – send your
Holy angels to join the choir
Of your children – singing your praise
One day heaven and earth sing
All glory and praise to you
Holy One – eternal God

Prayer Book Page 157

Thu, 12 May 2016 14:28:47

Eternal God, Jesus, Love
My love, a special prayer
From the children of the garden
To you Holy One – please fill their hearts
With your magnificent love – they pray

In thanksgiving, Holy One – every moment
Your family offers praise and glory
Receiving so many graces – embracing them
In peace – joy and love

Their songs see your sacred heart
Holy One – to be ever pleasing to you
One with you in all things – my love
Union with you is eternal – Holy One

There is no purpose before you
Or beyond you, Holy One
Without you only wandering in fear
Exists – in this prayer those who love you
Reach for you – love who exists forever
Love that lives for and in you Holy One
The only everlasting hope – of love
In this prayer they embrace you

Prayer Book Page 158

Fri, 20 May 2016 08:16:47

Eternal God, Jesus, Love
My love, the distance from here
To you is so great that the terrible things
Happening in the garden are not only forgotten
But obscures what is good so quickly

Suffering by such large numbers is so
Overwhelming the prayers of those suffering are
Suffocated as they wait for divine help
Waiting for you Holy One – to end the pain

My love – look at the children – crying
Bewildered by why the suffering goes on
Please Holy One, take away the distance
Between their suffering and your sacred heart

Most serious prayers constantly rise to you
Holy One – life all who suffer to a better place
Beside you – in your holiness – your kingdom
As evil seeks not only to destroy your church
But you as well

Please Holy One – gather the prayers of all who love you
All who live in your promises – they watch
Every day as evil gathers around them – destroying
All hope- through your love – it is time all
Who hate you now – Holy One – will continue hating you
Through their eternal agon

Prayer Book Page 159

Mon, 13 Jun 2016 11:37:49

Eternal God, Jesus, Love
My Lover, serious confusion
Sweeps the garden – snaring
Prayers without warning

Holy One, send your holy angels
To protect each prayer – carrying
Their love to embrace you
In your sacred heart

Holy One, let the power of your love
Reveal your glory – touching all
Who love you – hold them in
Your divine embrace – forgiving

Those who love you not only want you
To possess them – but want to possess
You also – to feel every breath of
Your being – all that you are – divine

My Love, this prayer seeks to hold your heart
Knowing you love them – waiting beyond
Every hour passing and coming – joined in
Your love – future divine – they know
You alone, Holy One – are the strength
Of their love, joy and peace – they know
Without you Holy One, there is no hope

Prayer Book Page 160

Thu, 16 Jun 2016 10:57:21

Eternal God, Jesus, Love
My Love, your children of the
Garden advancing in maturity
Pray with such love
Their souls move with such care
Ever close to you – desire gleaming

Please, Holy One – hold them near
Each prayer filled with love
A pure grace holds them
You give freely

My love, your children send their love
With every prayer from their lips
Separation from you is total pain
Please, Holy One – Embrace them in their prayer

There is a great longing in their heart
Seeking your love above all things
Every day the prayers of your children
Rise – filling the heavens with golden lights
Seeking peace for the end of the
Terrible agony in the garden
Tearing apart every heart
Your people

Prayer Book Page 161

Thu, 30 Jun 2016 13:40:17

Eternal God, Jesus, Love
My Love, how splendid when the
Early hours of each new day
Quietly carry the spirit in ecstasy
To places unknown collecting whispers
From the great ocean of your love

Holy One, the Lady in White
Your Mother, has arrived – standing alone
Weeping – for all the slaughtered babies
Together holding a bloody cross
I must go to her – take my place beside
Her – even die there
Sharing the pain and suffering
Shattering her heart – so many babies

Holy One, create anew this one in
Image and likeness – now one with you
Holy One – rising from your cross
Your magnificent love to join the
Lady in White in everlasting resurrection
Knowing all that was – all that will be
Now – in your divinity – still weeping
She knows one day you will return – Holy One
To condemn the garden – all will perish
The good and the bad, there will be
Established in heaven a place for the babies
To cry for all eternity for their mothers

Prayer Book Page 162

Sun, 31 Jul 2016 14:00:56

Eternal God, Jesus, Love
My Love, this prayer to give thanks
On behalf of all the children
In the garden – who love you Holy One
And cannot let pass – so many gifts
Of your holy love – pure gifts – graces

Holy One, this prayer – a living prayer
Thank you for so many days of joy
Known by all in the garden

Thank you Holy One for peace
The world cannot give
Such goodness is from your heart – only

Thank you Holy One – for the Eucharist
Being there in union – every day – we live

All in the garden – who love you
Know and hold the truth – your father
Through the Holy Spirit – took to himself
Every wound, every pain – every sorrow
And every suffering inflicted upon you - His Son
In the agony of your passion, the agony of
Your crucifixion – the agony of your death
He knew it all – Holy One you brought the gift
Resurrection – in the Father's burst of divine love

Prayer Book Page 163

Sat, 06 Aug 2016 21:20:31

Eternal God, Jesus, Love
My Love, as you search my heart
See if anything has been denied to you
As all that is there belongs to you

Holy One, listen to the voice of my heart
Surely you can hear only your name
Spoken softly – in a whisper
The voice calls for you – alone

My love – my heart waits for you
As my spirit weeps to hear
Your voice embracing – comforting
The light of you – takes away the pain
Of separation

Holy One, bring back those
Special moments when the grace of you
Filled my heart with everlasting love

My Love, knowing there is no life beyond you
Touch this heart – fill it with your love
Nothing else is needed – in the eternal light
Of you – life blossoms – come now
Claim my heart to be in union with your own

Pruyer Book Page 164

Mon, 15 Aug 2016 10:21:41

Eternal God, Jesus, Love
My Love, this prayer is
Holy One – Restoration

Angels weep for restoration
Of spirit of the children of the garden
Hearts empty – dark – horrifying
For you Holy One

Restoration, My Love, something
Is missing from every heart
You, Holy One, can promote
Restoration to every heart

What then do your children seek
My Love, what is it they seek
From your heart, Holy One
Your children call for the restoring
Of Hope – living without hope
Is crying for death

Please, Holy One, empty every heart
Of darkness and grant to all
The grace of irreplaceable hope
Every life has to live in hope
You alone, My Love, are the truth of hope

Prayer Book Page 165

Thu, 25 Aug 2016 15:38:40

Eternal God, Jesus, Love
My Love, there is severe suffering
In the garden, so many of your
Children live in great sorrow

Holy One – please come back
Dispel from every hear the darkness
Your children weep
Not understanding why they suffer

The quiet times are no more
No singing can be heard – joy has faded
My Love – your children wonder
Are they expected to live without you

Angelic whispers pass over the garden
Seeking the peace of what once was
The children are a flame in the dust of
Joy meant to be

Holy One – come back soon
Your children wait for one word
To fil the empty hours
With grace – love – peace

Prayer Book Page 166

Mon, 05 Sep 2016 21:09:07

Eternal God, Jesus, Love
My Love, more longing rising
Your children in the garden
Sending their love – in prayers

Holy One – your children know
You love them – across the great distance
The challenge against faith
That must remain very powerful

My Love – much help is needed
There is a great mountain of hate
The garden seeks to move beyond self
Into oneness with you – salvation

Holy One – Please know – our prayers
Reach to you – how wonderful it is
To hold you in spirit in knowing
How you love all of us – the depths of each soul

Eternal – Holy One – your children
Offer a simple prayer into everlasting
Thanking you for the magnificent joy
Being with you – receiving your love

Prayer Book Page 167

Wed, 21 Sep 2016 14:58:06

Eternal God, Jesus, Love
My love, your children are
Whispering among themselves
As confusion is mounting - painfully

Holy One - conflict between freewill
which you gave to all - and things
being heard from those in high position
of your church - confusion
you should return Holy One and recapture
your church and restore truth

My love you are the only truth
It does seem sometimes - errors
spring up - in careless ways
your children are left to confusion

Who speaks the truth
to your children wandering aimless
spirits filled with pain - empty - sorrow
confusion difficult to absorb

Pray now every day - for peace
in the soul there is only one to be trusted
People in white are not always
Proclaimed - saints - ordinary people are first

Prayer Book Page 168

Eternal God, Jesus, Love
My Love, waiting for stones
To cry out your name and shed tears
The suffering is so severe

Return Holy One, Let your Holy Spirit
Renew the garden in your splendor
And Glory – heal your children – in love
There seems to be no end – terrible suffering

Come back Holy One – so many dying
Explosions rip apart the garden
Sending so many into your kingdom
There seems to be preference for evil

Continuous echoes of pain reach
Your kingdom – Holy One please recover the garden
Turn out evil ones – joining in pain
End the darkness with your divine light

My love – terrible things are happening
Day after day – evil prevails
Only you Holy One can bring the light
Of your love home – as wise men of great position
Are unable to bring peace to the garden
Maybe the wise men don't want to end the suffering

Prayer Book Page 169

Wed, 12 Oct 2016 12:53:37

Eternal God, Jesus, Love
My love, into your sacred heart
This prayer is placed – forever
To be captured in your love

The children – Holy One – your babies
Being destroyed by evil choices
Their innocence – no longer sacred
Dying – by brutal desire – suffering

Please, Holy One, call them to be with you
In your Kingdom let them grow
And prosper without pain
Living with you without suffering

Be their joy – Fill their hearts
So tiny – with your splendid love
Living in you forever
In your embrace – children of the garden

When my love – will the slaughter end
Tearing apart you babies
The fires of hell wait for all those
Who complete the slaughter
And one day they will all listen to the
Cries endured by millions of babies
Listen they will for all eternity – to the pain
And suffering they inflicted

Prayer Book Page 170

Fri, 28 Oct 2016 13:44:57

Eternal God, Jesus, Love
My love, this prayer direct
To your heart
For such a long time

Periodically, prayers speak of the
Lady in White, your Mother
Known as the Mother of God
An enormous change has to be accepted
Mother to be divine
Can it be Mother has been given divinely

To be the Immaculate Conception
Is very special – without sin
Is to be Divine – how beautiful
Mother is your right hand Holy One

Not so brilliant this one - your servant Holy One
Just seems sometimes we forget
Your Mother – who is really is
Most likely elevated into Divinity
Her participation blessed by you
Holy One – Magnificent Love
The Lady in White - Divine

Prayer Book Page 171

Eternal God, Jesus, Love
My Love, for your sacred heart – Holy One
There never seems to be
Enough time to pray

The mind is too active
Spirit is lost in nonsense
Trying to fix itself
To focus on you Holy One

How to cope with spiritual
Loneliness – holding on to you
My love is not easy – constant effort
Is required – losing self in prayer

How nice to hear angels singing
Watching time passing – day to day
The garden filling with tears
Sorrowful seeking nearness – to your cross

My Love, your children in the garden
Are suffering beyond their hours
If prayers – reaching for you
Seeking the peace – only you can give

Prayer Book Page 172

Fri, 11 Nov 2016 13:43:15

Eternal God, Jesus, Love
My Love, this special prayer
Is to embrace your sacred heart
Holy One – your magnificent love

My Love, let your angels fill the garden
With prayerful singing – joyfully
Lifting the darkness of pain and
Suffering – holding every heart – peacefully

Your children in the garden
Long to embrace you in their love
Just to be with you each day
Separation is known to be so painful

So many want simply to spend
Each day with you – belong to you
Just knowing your love – is all
Holy One, come back – give your children – you

My Love time – wasted easily
When your return is all desire
Please, Holy One – reach every heart
Your love on the cross – begins eternal life

Prayer Book Page 173

Fri, 18 Nov 2016 13:35:10

Eternal God, Jesus, Love
My Love, in the midst of pain
And suffering in spirit
You spoke - your name was spoken
In union only joy – perfect joy

Holy One, no matter the way of the
Spirit, union gave hope eternal – suffering
Is dissolved in you – the moment is
Taken into your love – new strength
Provides the bridge to your
Everlasting kingdom - a place prepared
For faith to live in eternal expansion

Holy One, in the midst of pain and suffering
You were held – in that moment
You held the pain and suffering
Completing the moment – for flight
Into your sacred will

Holy One, bringing to mind
Your own pain and suffering of salvation - beyond understanding
We learn how your divine mercy
Calls to freedom the suffering soul
Into the sweetness and pure joy
Of your love

Prayer Book Page 174

Tue, 06 Dec 2016 20:42:47

Eternal God Jesus Love
My Love, this prayer seeks
to find you in your terrible suffering
On the cross - there in your silence
Find the answer as to - Why?

How could you allow such agony
to inflame every thought in your mind
allowing terrible instruments of torture to
embrace your heart and soul

Holy One - Share the scourging
The crowned thorns - pierced hands and feet
Share the sorrow with those who love you
Let each hour condemn - such pain and suffering

This prayer Holy One - submerges
Imperfect love - deep into the wounded
Magnificent love of your cross

This prayer seeks to find the avenue
leading to sharing every wound
Every pain endured on you - Holy One
The only way to be one with you

All who love you - Holy One
will find protection in union with you

Prayer Book Page 175

Mon, 12 Dec 2016 20:01:32

Eternal God, Jesus, Love

My Love, the Lady in White

Arrived unexpectedly, dream

Or vision, understanding - beyond abilities

In the glow of absolute purity and

Holiness, the night was devoured

As Her glorious light consumed the darkness

Holy One, spirit came to life

As sweet singing reached soul

From far away, elevation mixed with tears

Impossible to speak - words frozen

Resting in her light - her purity

Beyond being defined - joy prevailed

Holy One, this prayer carries a

New magnificent love

Splendidly beautiful moments do no last

Dark of night returned - the Lady was gone

Surly this was a dream

Where life was to rest forever

My Love, send the Lady back - full of grace

Let brief moments of love - continue

Lady of the resurrection - perfect love

Grant another dream - Holy One - Just one more

Prayer Book Page 176

Fri, 23 Dec 2016 00:45:26

Eternal God, Jesus, Love

My Love, Where have all

The rainbows gone, Holy One

In the garden so many children

Crying - so many children dying

How is it possible, Holy One

For such carnage to be

The truth of each new day

Bombs exploding - tearing life away

Stark eyes stare - as

The slaughter goes on

Where have the rainbows gone

No more children singing

See the garden caught in flashes

sending dark billows - debris rising

Babies bodies flying

No one can stop - the slaughtering

Holy One - this prayer pleads

For you eternal one to call the

Dying to yourself - for life

Leave the doers of death - to

Eternal darkness - the second death

Why are all the churches empty - closed

Where are the prayers reaching

What has happened to happiness - is the garden dying

Prayer Book Page 177

Fri, 30 Dec 2016 00:44:35

Eternal God, Jesus, Love
My Love, how wonderful to speak
Your holy name in prayer
Knowing you love every word
That carries our love to you

In prayer, we are close to you
A union that allows us to feel
Your embrace receiving so many gifts
Of your love through every prayer

How wonderful it is to give
What is received from you
To others – the gifts of your love
To those sick and suffering

They remain unknown to us – prayers reach
Holy One – filled with love – as you hold them
A gift to them – from a loving heart
Your compassion – healing love

Nothing is so good as sending you your love
In caving humble prayer to those in great need
Knowing your heart will capture them
As you give them your magnificent love on the cross

Why are so many churches empty
No prayers being offered – where are the children
Send your love – bring them home

Prayer Book Page 178

Tue, 17 Jan 2017 21:57:12

Eternal God, Jesus, Love
My Love, there was a young lady
Who, very mysteriously became
Your Mother – visited by a glorious angel
All that was needed were her words
"Be it done" – miracles begin

Her name is Mary – spoken throughout heaven
This young lady – knew great sorrows
Were pending – no hesitation – stepping
Forward in the mystery – she embraced each moment

Voices angrily shouted for crucifixion
Death their only way – where did
Such anger come from – only yesterday
He healed them – now lost – they wanted his blood

Some wept – others shouted crucify him
She lived in his pain and suffering
So many hearts closed – nails were struck
The King of Creation – a common criminal

Her name is Mary – soul filling with each new sorrow
Collecting His blood in her robes
She knew well her baby was dying
His cross became her cross
The promised sword pierced her soul sharply
Her blood mixed with that of her son
Eternal union in sorrow - completed

Prayer Book Page 179

Fri, 03 Feb 2017 16:28:26

Eternal God, Jesus, Love
My Love, Spirit weeps in
Darkness, gripped in profound
Human capacity

The question, Holy One, is not
So much why but how –
How did you endure so much
Beginning to end – nailed to the wood

No matter – strength of effort
Understanding no forthcoming
To hear only silence – groans
As you passed by

When you fell – your suffering was not
Only heard but felt – by all
Reaching for you no amount of
Tears could change the moment –
Turning away – hatred

The price of salvation
Truly very high – measured in blood

Prayer Book Page 180

Fri, 24 Feb 2017 12:54:04

Eternal God, Jesus, Love
My love, so many distractions flow
In and out of the Garden – moving
Spirit in troubling ways

The only source of peace
Is you – Holy One – only you to trust
Only you to turn to in such times
Only through you Holy One – can spirit find rest

Holy One – can you let it be
That we can walk together
Let life have its proper meaning
Beyond all distractions of the world

At times of weariness, my love
Will you be there and let us rest
To hold on to you to be
Strengthened and renewed

There is no one else to reach for
You are the only truth
You alone are the life
Of all love – touching
And embracing eternity

Prayer Book Page 182

Sun, 26 Mar 2017 23:28:52
Eternal God, Jesus, Love
My Love, every day spirit
Seeks divine nourishment
Found only in the Eucharist

You Holy One are eternal food
That spirit seeks in all afflictions
Only in you my love can spirit live
Nourished in your flesh and blood

My love, how is it some live
Without you, not knowing – even
One thought of eternal life
The world is everything – to so many in the garden

So many in need – to pray for
To be presented to you – through prayer
Grant the mercy of your magnificent love
Heal them Holy One – End suffering

My love – the garden is filled
With terrible suffering – no end in sight
Please return – great the peace only you
Can give – let the warmth of your reign
And be supreme in every heart

Prayer Book Page 183

Thu, 06 Apr 2017 22:13:04

Eternal God, Jesus, Love
My Love, waiting for you
Holy One is mystery itself
Just to hear your voice
Calling my name – Glory
Above all Glory

Looking into your eyes
Holy One- ends all mystery
Speaking together – eternal love
Union – creates forever – by God alone

My Love, How many times
Have I looked at you
Suffering, hanging on that
Terrible cross, with only one
Desire in my heart – to take you
Down and hold you – share your wounds, pain

Holy One, the joy of you
Prevails over al pain and suffering
Only you can embrace each heart
Yielding true love - ever lasting – happiness

My Love – please provide a path
That leads directly to your cross
Allow us to hold you – take down
Share your suffering here in the garden

Prayer Book Page 184

Fri, 21 Apr 2017 16:26:05

Eternal God, Jesus, Love,
My Love, How is it – that so many
Have such difficulty believing
In you – your cross should be enough

To believers – no day begins or
Ends with reaching for you
Knowing that without doubt
The nearness and presence of you

Every believer feels a great sorrow
For those who turn away from you
Never knowing the joy of you
Please Holy One – give them your magnificent love

My Love – in the wash of grace
Seeing the Lady in White – your mother
So very sad – carrying the weapons
Of crucifixion – thorns and nails for
Such a long time – an offering was made
But she did not accept the
Offering – but held firmly the sorrow
The suffering and the pain of the weapons
Peace can only be found in your Holy Spirit

Prayer Book Page 185

Thu, 25 May 2017 18:09:13

Eternal God, Jesus, Love
My love, walking the long path
My friend, unknown along with me
Sometimes speaking then silent
Now and then stopping me with light
The way is long with my friend unknown

Sometimes the light is very strong
Speaking softly – especially when close
Warming my being in ways
Physical and in ways spiritual

There is a continuous awareness
Walking with my friend in the light
Care is given lest I be carried
Well beyond my capacity

My friend tells me many things
Through the light – great love – peace
Living love – consuming me joyfully
Only in the purest love can spirit
Exist in the light – soon days
Will end – spirit is ready

Prayer Book Page 186

Thu, 25 May 2017 18:13:39

Eternal God, Jesus, Love
My love, realization reached
The extend of evil in the garden
Terrible – we can only pray
Welcome into your kingdom – Holy One
All those evil – has hurt

There is no turning away
Or ignoring the sorrow
Being inflicted – no one is
Beyond the evil touch
Hell is waiting – to consume
The servants of evil

Why can't we know
The children of Satan
Who wait in the darkness
To murder – finding their
Way into the fires of hell

Holy One – grant your truly
Magnificent love and divine mercy
To all who are hurt by evil's
Servants – they will spend eternity
In darkness – unable to even see
You Holy One – as you embrace
And give life to those who have been hurt

Prayer Book Page 187

Thu, 22 Jun 2017 15:19:54

Eternal God, Jesus Love,
My Love, How often have I
Wondered about extent of the
pain and suffering filing each day

How long, Holy One
Has spirit suffered to find
A way to thank you for your
Magnificent love - of healing

It is realized that simply
saying, "Thank you" is not rough
and does not in any way
Reach the embrace of you

Holy One, spirit suffers not being
Able to serve you - to be your servant
To comfort you against the rants
of those who do not love you

Spirit knows - no one deserves
Love more than you - Holy One
Your love is pure
The love of spirit is imperfect

Spirit feels useless - not serving
Through many days of prayer
Your glory and power - remaining true
And overwhelming - unto everlasting life

Prayer Book Page 188

Mon, 10 Jul 2017 22:21:09

Eternal God, Jesus, Love
My Love - so many times
spirit - rests in the garden
Offered to all in the garden
by servants of darkness

Holy One - how can it be
Seeing suffering - crushing the hearts
Of your children - as they become cold
Moving distant without prayer

My Love - how is it possible
So many lose sight of you
There is no warmth for souls
Aimlessly reaching for you - your love

My Love - search harsh understanding
When your children are enriched
With spiritual loneliness without love
Distance increasing - your touch - is love lost

My love - please - returning we know nothing
Can replace you there is no life without you
Holy One - without you nothing can exist
Your love gives life - even to the wind

Prayer Book Page 189

Thu, 27 Jul 2017 23:17:39

Eternal God, Jesus, Love
My love, please know Holy One
So many of your children
Have perished in the garden
For your love - after living in hope

Holy One - This prayer cries for
Your compassion reaching into your heart
To hold fast your love - forever
But to find compelling love
In your heart forever

My Love - this prayer calls you back
To the garden waiting for your embrace
For all abandoned praying for you
To hold them
Calling them to your kingdom

Holy One, slaying the innocent
Seeing to them comes so easily for souls
Filled with evil - satanic
Only you, Holy One, can end the slaughter
Send your love to each soul
Martyred by their hands and
Hearts filled with evil

Prayer Book Page 190

Wed, 02 Aug 2017 22:51:46

Eternal God, Jesus, Love
My love, reaching for your
Heart, your love is not easy
Knowing how many voices hold
You in love - as their hearts break

Holy One - Take their words
Into your heart - keep them in your
Divine mercy - compassion
So many hearts cry in suffering

Holy One - Please lead the way
To peach - Divine compassion
Hold each soul in eternal healing Lord
No suffering too small to leave unattended

My Love, spirit weeps in the children of the garden
Suffering is escalating - pain so distinctive
One time all could speak your name
No matter the pain - one is calling

My Love, how can your children
Find peace - without you - never
Only you - Holy One - can command
quiet and calm - only you my love can create peace

My love, your children are desperate
For healing - only you can give

Prayer Book Page 191

Wed, 09 Aug 2017 21:24:21

Eternal God, Jesus, Love
My love, spirit knows after
Endless days of praying
No one but you Holy One is worthy of
The trust born of faith

Every prayer sends pure love
To you Holy One - not loosely spoken
Or carelessly offered - especially
When offered for someone in deep need

Prayers offered for someone unknown
Especially welcomed - made whole
By your love - Holy One - as suffering souls
Many times cannot cry out for themselves

Prayer - Holy One is union with you
In which imperfect love is made perfect
Only in your does prayer have meaning
Embraced in divine healing and compassion

Only loving hearts can spend long hours
In caring prayers for those in need
Holy One - You know suffering is so real
Man cannot speak your name in their suffering
Please Holy One - open your heart let the
Pain and suffering rush in - calling you
And you magnificent love to embrace prayers
Now being spoken - for so many

Prayer Book Page 192

Wed, 16 Aug 2017 21:20:30

Eternal God, Jesus, Love
My Love, spirit knows clearly
There is only one desire for the soul
Only you - Holy one - no other desire
Fills his heart - you Holy One - only you

Spirit longs for your kingdom
To be embraced in your divine love
Spirit knows there is no death
Only resurrection through you - Holy One

Spirit tries always to understand
Without success - the extent of your
Passion and death on the cross - death defeated
Spirit can only ask - how did you do it
Passing into silence - such pain and suffering

In love - spirit can love only you
To obtain your magnificent love on the cross
There is no one to be loved - beyond you
Holy One - all is complete in you

Holy One - come back - give your love
To all reaching for you - in holy prayer
Let those who pray to you - live in you
In your love - beyond all that is
Beginning and ending - Suffering for you Holy One

Prayer Book Page 193

Mon, 28 Aug 2017 20:59:17

Eternal God, Jesus, Love
My Love, Holy One, spirit is
Struggling to understand
How long the pain and suffering is 9/11 to be endured

How many times does the soul
reach through crumbling buildings
Before consolation both in the spiritual
And material words is found
Knowing it comes only through you, Holy One

Where is comfort found - when all that is
Left of a loved one - is a piece of bone
A loved one is gone - to mix with
The debris of exploding buildings

Where is the peace - found in prayer
Knowing two survived while another
Died in the evil attack - Desire turned to revenge

Surely Holy One - such anger
Cannot live in the hearts of those
Living in you and for you - it is known
Peace can only be obtained through you
Holy One - Hold the fallen - those
Who were destroyed by the actions
Of evil people - satanic members of death.\\

Prayer Book Page 194

Sun, 10 Sep 2017 01:32:29

Eternal God, Jesus, Love
My Love, some special things
Can't do, first - can't live without you
to be that way is to be dead
Knowing on emptiness

Can't understand the terrible hatred
That caused your suffering leading to your crucifixion
How was it possible for you to
Endure so much so calmly

Can't live each day without
Moments of silence in prayer
Can't understand why this
Spirit was born a sinner

Can't understand your magnificent love
No matter what you give
Freely every moment of life
Knowing my love is so imperfect

Holy One - so many things I can't do
Yet reaching for you - perfect love
Is never ending - giving spirit life
Happiness - fulfillment - joy

Prayer Book Page 195

Eternal God, Jesus, Love
My Love, so many days
Arrive bringing distress
With so many sick – barely alive
Seeing them – the children – so difficult

Only prayer – to you – Holy One
Brings peace – needed so much
Reaching for you Holy One – not easy
Prayer is the bridge – sinner to God

Holy One – so often spirit feels
You are so afar away – praying the only way
To cross the distance to hold you
You are the highest good – Love

Who are we that you should receive
Our prayers – we see the joy of you
We depend on your love
To calm the fears building – each day

When Holy One – When we can embrace
Holding you in our imperfect love
Little consolation – not reaching you
It is not easy – we wait for you – love
To answer the sincere prayers – of longing hearts
Please Holy One accept the love and gratitude
Spirit offers to my Love for the grace of healing here
You gave to someone very special

Prayer Book Page 196

Wed, 20 Sep 2017 21:55:40

Eternal God, Jesus, Love
My Love, there is one - so
Forgotten -the Holy Spirit
The one who gives everything to all of us

How to say thank you
For the gift of love every day
We are in such need of the spirit
Holy One guide us in prayer

There seems to be no limits
Holy One to the reaching of the spirit
We pray to be lifted up in Him
Finding understanding in His grace

We pray to the giver of life
For the sweet joy of peace and love
To walk with Him
Knowing the truth of love   peace

Holy One - we pray for you
To send the Holy Spirit to help us
To just live - each day
In Holy ways hat are beyond us

Prayer Book Page 197

Eternal God, Jesus, Love
My Love, every day pausing
In quiet prayer – for you
To come here – to be the moment
That fills the heart – with magnificent love

My Love, through long hours
Prayers that lead to visits
With you – where wisdom
is imparted to your servant

Holy One – with you life is full
Knowing how you care about us
We are carried through each day
By your magnificent love – eternal

How beautiful is it to be with you
Holy One – to feel your presence
And to engage your spirit
In the sounds of angels singing

So wonderful – time in prayer
Where the warmth of you
Embraces spirit's soul
And all that is divine consumes
What is human

Prayer Book Page 198

Mon, 02 Oct 2017 22:48:40

Eternal God, Jesus, Love
My Love, there are times when
It is so easy to hear the silence
In prayers reaching for you

A real sadness arrives upon
Seeing how many leave you
to never again hold you
In Love - in their prayers

Souls who leave you
No longer sing - pray with longing
To hold you - what has happened
Terrible emptiness grips them = voices die
Without prayer

Where are you - my love - eternal
No praying is life - without hope
Hearts unable to sing - joining
Holy angels prayers building - paths to heaven

Forgetting about you - ending true life
Giving nothing of self - love in prayer
One in you - eternal prayer divine gift of love
Every prayer offered to your sacred heart
Holy One - bring the warmth of you ever closer

Prayer Book Page 199

Mon, 09 Oct 2017 19:17:18

Eternal God, Jesus, Love
My Love, so many times I forget
To pray for a special grace
The grace of your mercy - Holy One

Spirit, knows - Holy One - When given in prayer
The grace of your mercy in everything
Healing love, compassion - all graces
Can be found in your mercy - how wonderful

The prayer of this day - not for spirit
But for all in need of your mercy
To the freedom from suffering
From pain - the need is great - waiting

Please Holy One let the flame
Of your divine mercy burn bright
Forever in the heart of spirit
Born everlasting love - purifying

Prayer is offered to you Holy One
In thanksgiving for your mercy
For understanding - holding you
Being one - divine mercy - eternal

Prayer Book Page 200

Sat, 14 Oct 2017 01:33:47

Eternal God, Jesus, Love
My Love, please Holy One
Grant a special grace of love
To all Who read the prayers
Of the book being forward

Engulf each reader in the fullness of your love
Abandon yourself in each heart
Reaching for you - be the light they need
The peace that only you can give

This prayer calls you Holy One
To hold each reader - seeking you
Joining their love with you - eternally with you

Please Holy One unite your being
With each soul reaching for you in prayer
To be with you eternally in prayer
In one love divine - bless them
Let them know you are the with them

Prayer Book Page 201

Tue, 07 Nov 2017 21:40:48

Eternal God, Jesus, Love
My Love, often wondered
What will come after – prayers to you
Holy One – every abortion – how can it be
Such an evil lives – as life dies

Life or death choices – by some many – against so many
Casually chosen as the tiny voice – cry – let me live
You have lived into full being
Why not let me live in the misery of being

For years – voices cried out – it's murder
Then quiet covered all – so many do it – leave it alone
Remaining voices covered in quiet
Faded saying nothing – either way

So many souls suffer – in the face of silence
We all did with each mother – sharing
Please Holy One – remember all – found in
Trash cans – still breathing – holding on
To life – breathing in your resurrection

To each tiny body that will be given
Holy One – surely you know each by name
When you ask Holy One – why – why
Babies given to life – when you arrive go and
Stay with your baby – another choice has to be made

Prayer Book Page 202

Tue, 07 Nov 2017 21:43:19

Eternal God, Jesus, Love
My Love – there are times
When subject matter is very difficult
To consider – but still requires prayers

The prime subject today being
Considered is abortion – not easy
Very often filled pain and relief
Depending upon the user – view

If one billion souls make the choice
Do you Holy One say "alright"
Turn away – praying – doing nothing
With the billion dead babies – all is alright

Will you Holy One welcome one billion
Who have destroyed their babies
And call of them into your kingdom
Then turn to the babies - as a passing event

What is that Holy One – a baby speaks and
Say what it is mother coming – something to say
He wants his mother to stay with him
There is still another choice to be made

Prayer Book Page 203

Sat, 18 Nov 2017 16:44:26

Eternal God, Jesus, Love
My Love, Holy One a great
Loneliness devours spirit
Leaving spirit in terrible darkness

It is true Holy One - when you are
Not close - Spirit feels deeply - separation
And understand how you are needed
As spirit suffers your absence

Once holding you in love Holy One
No n love Holy One
It comes a requirement for daily living
Once within you a divine love
agony takes your place - huge separation

Nothing can equal the love you give
Living in the spirit of you
No enjoyment can surpass
the joy of you - your angels
Spirit speaks joyfully - happiness with you.

You alone Holy One offer eternal life
To live to the full with you - forever
This prayer is offered for continuing
The union of spirit and eternity forever

Prerayer Book Page 204

Tue, 21 Nov 2017 17:24:53

Eternal God, Jesus, Love
My Love, this must be the prayer
Offered to you - Holy One for the
Many sick - so many dying

Prayers that seek you to be with them
As they suffer terrible pain
Sometimes in silence - reaching for you
Holy One - sometimes not so quiet agony

Please - Holy One - hold those close to you
Who are suffering and dying
Let pain suffered received your
Magnificent love gracefully - on the cross

This prayer then is for them
Lift those suffering pain and sorrow
Into your divinity - to obtain peace
As only you can give - understanding their suffering
Through each passing day

Holy One - eternal God - you alone can
fill each spirit with unending love
Show them your caring - take all of their suffering
Freeing each soul to find peace in you alone.

Prayer Book Page 205

Eternal God, Jesus, Love
My Love, considering the distance
Between us and the silence that
Resounds day after day

This prayer is offered Holy One
For all who are taken from us
By evil people in numbers
That are struggling and sorrowful

Please Holy One gather them
To your Sacred Heart and
Give them your abundant love
Rescue them from suffering

Let this prayer reach you on their behalf
Fill their souls with your light
Open the eyes of their souls
To be in your glory

Prayer is the best we can offer
On their behalf - Our love heals them
Prayerfully we keep them in spirit
Beliving you Holy One love them forever

Prayer Book Page 206

Tue, 12 Dec 2017 21:26:06

Eternal God, Jesus, Love
My Love, this prayer offered to you
Holy One on behalf of the millions
Of tiny creatures in your image and likeness
Discarded as nothing more than
Scraps of garbage torn from the womb of life

These millions created in your
Image and likeness no longer
Talking to you in the womb - having been
murdered by the pleasure that
culled them into being - no longer
living in desire - pleasure
Have new names in angelic arms

The future stands in darkness
bitter destruction
Thou divine love
There will be no peace
until the slaughter ends
The weeping of the tiny ones
will last until the end of time

Prayer Book Page 207

Sat, 23 Dec 2017 00:40:04

Eternal God, Jesus, Love
My Love this prayer Holy One
Is to enter into your sacred heart
Bring to mind, the fullness of your suffering

To give every heart
The agony of your crucifixion
Allowing no one to forget
The full measure of your sacrifice
The full measure of your love

Every wound brought into focus
the reality of eternal life
The reality of how short the span
of Life in this world

A serious and bitter darkness
Grips many hearts - drawing them away
from you Holy One - into loss of holiness
Weeping for what was - peace
Peace that you alone can give

In love
With love
For Love

Spirit is reaching for you
Holy One
The only love worth
Living and dying for

Prayer Book Page 208

Wed, 01 Aug 2018 08:49:16

Eternal God, Jesus love
This prayer is lifted to you, Holy One, on behalf of all the sick
children
hoping that your healing will reach them

So many of them perish
As there is no one to pray for them

Looking into expressionless faces
Eyes staring, pleading for hope
One can feel their sorrow and suffering, Holy One

Time passes without mercy, taking the souls of the sick children
Only prayer can embrace them with their needs, Holy One
in their passing

Love becomes supreme for all,
because of you, Holy One

Prayer Book Page 209

Tue, 14 Aug 2018 13:17:23

Eternal God, Jesus, Love,
My love, reaching for your heart, Holy One,
And Magnificent healing love,
Rising with the angels in loving care
For all the sick and wounded

Please, Holy One, see the suffering
of the many who reach for you
Living in hope of finding peace
in the chaos now taking hold of them

Holy One, in your arms the wounded
Find peace and comfort knowing
The grace of your mercy in theirs

Prayer Book Page 210

Tue, 21 Aug 2018 15:21:58

Eternal God, Jesus, Love
My Love, this prayer is offered
To you, Holy One, on behalf of
Sixty million plus innocents slaughtered
The slaughter continues. Forming bodies
are torn apart and discarded as
garbage. Faith reveals they have a soul.

Please, Holy One, call to yourself
The broken and destroyed. Call
the murderess hands to witness their destruction
Judge severely all those
who have ignored your command "not to kill"
In your kingdom give life to all the babies destroyed
"the fires of hell are burning bright"

Prayer Book Page 211

Mon, 10 Sep 2018 10:14:13

Eternal God, Jesus, Love
My Love, it is time to ay thank you
For your most important gift - the gift
Of your presence in the Holy Eucharist.
Your body, blood, soul and divinity in
The Holy Eucharist. We live because of this
Gift of your love

At this time, the seeds of hate have
Blossomed, suffocating divine healing,
Love and mercy. Reaching to you,
Holy One, for peace, the heart lies in
Darkness, hoping for your light
To give life.

Bless those, Holy One, who keep your
Commandment, "not to kill" admonish
those who have ignored your will and
Participated in the slaughter of
Children

Prayer Book Page 212

Tue, 02 Oct 2018 16:48:39

Eternal God, Jesus, Love,
My Love, Overwhelming lonelines
captures the soul reaching for you
Holy One, desire to be one with
divinity becomes difficult when
separation is understood and
experienced. Those who never
reach for the light will never know
the warmth of divine love
Thos who live prayerfully in
the light will see the face of God

Prayer Book Page 213

Tue, 09 Oct 2018 12:38:15

Eternal God, Jesus, Love
My Love, your Godly silence
is profoundly known when
Prayers are spoken for those
Who need them. Prayers
Seemingly go against your divine intentions
It is difficult to understand what
Seems to be silent rejection

Much is given to your saints, Holy One.
In their love for you they
Suffer in grace. We
Endure in our suffering, and
In our prayers we lose the moment,
As spirit flees.

Prayer Book Page 214

Thu, 08 Nov 2018 11:51:20

Eternal God, Jesus, Love,
My Love, This prayer is lifted
To you, Holy One, on behalf of
Those souls reaching for you
and the warmth of your love.

Loving souls gather at your
Cross, Holy One, weeping in pain
and sorrow, sharing agony of
your passion

Standing in your light from
The cross sharing the agony of
Your passion. Sorrow is given
To souls who love you. All live
In grace of the gift of the
Resurrection.

Prayer Book Page 215

Thu, 08 Nov 2018 11:54:30

Eternal God, Jesus, Love
My Love, this prayer is given to you
To console your heart each time
You see those who come to your cross
And walk away abandoning you.

The great sadness you must feel seeing
Them walk away abandoning your
Gift of sacrifice.

Surely, Holy One, you feel
Great sadness each time a
Soul turns away from the light
Of your sacrifice on the cross

This prayer is to return to you
The love of the horror
Of the cross. In the mystery
Of your magnificent love we exist.

Prayer Book Page 216

Thu, 08 Nov 2018 11:56:35

Eternal God, Jesus, Love
My Love, this prayer is centered
In your sacred heart on the cross.

In every wound this prayer
Reaches for your healing love
And divine mercy

Remembering all the sick and
Dying sharing in your sorrow
And suffering of your cross

Holy One, embrace all those
Who walk to your cross of
Sorrow. Call all of them to be
One with you as you are one
With the Father.

Prayer Book Page 217

Tue, 15 Jan 2019 12:06:23

Eternal God, Jesus, Love
My Love, This prayer is
Lifted to you, Holy One, to your
Sacred heart as you suffer
On the cross.

We pray you will
Welcome all souls into your
Kingdom, especially those
Who have suffered

To those who have suffered through
the years of life and find themselves
in despair unable to share your suffering
Call them by name, so they know of
your caring. Lift them up through
the sanctuary of your love

Prayer Book Page 218

Tue, 15 Jan 2019 12:11:19

Eternal God, Jesus, Love
My Love, this prayer is lifted
to you, Holy One, as we wait in
Hope you will remember the sick
And the dying. In your mercy
Grant your love to each
In fervent prayer reaching
For you Holy One, we see
Your light dispel the darkness
That hides us from you
And the loneliness that consumes
Us in the fear of knowing we
are not in passion of you
We are ready to share
With you the agony of your
passion of the Cross of Salvation

Prayer Book Page 220

Tue, 15 Jan 2019 12:14:04

Eternal God, Jesus, Love
My Love, Prayerfully receive
For you each day must be
Calm and in silence so that
The talking between the divine
And the soul can be completed
Or else the Flowers of peace
And healing love cannot
Blossom in the chaos and
Conflict of the ordinary life
Only When the soul is consumed in
Divinity can triumph be declared on
The part of the soul. Prayer has to
Be constant for the elevation of the
Soul. Faith has to be nourished
To foster calm and healing love
Darkness is swept
Away in the grace of divine
Love. True happiness can
Only be found in the divine union
The human heart will remain
Lonesome until it is secure
In your hands, Holy One.

Prayer Book Page 221

Tue, 15 Jan 2019 12:18:08

Eternal God, Jesus, Love
My Love, Reaching for you to take
Hold of you is not easy due
To the space between us.
Desire dictates how one feels about
Not being able to complete
The task most desirable is the wish
To share your suffering.
Every day distractions serve
Only to dilute inspirations
Of faith. We find we are
Unable to join in union
with you, Holy One
We are entirely too busy
To grasp the significance of
Prayerful intent in the Love
Of God.

Prayer Book Page 223

Sat, 02 Feb 2019 14:29:42

Eternal God, Jesus Love

My love, in reverence approaching your Cross, hoping to share your Passion, we reach to you with love, we recognize the brutality of your crucifixion when we pray it is "thy will be done as it is in heaven." To violate God's law is opening the door to hell.

Please, Holy One, enlighten us to the mystery of salvation and Resurrection. In Your supreme love, we find peace and joy. Through the storms of life, which are plenty, we can take refuge in the Eucharist.

How often does the perpetrator of darkness come to steal the peace and joy from you Holy One, leaving in our heart disquiet and anxiety. It is not enough to simply pray. We have to hold to You because of the power we have to face from the perpetrator. In our weakness, the darkness can triumph.

Prayer Book Page 224

Wed, 06 Feb 2019 11:34:01

Eternal God, Jesus, Love,
My Love, When I was born, Holy One,
I was ignorant of you and your sacrifice,
But now, I have grown and I am able to stand
Here in front of you and
Contemplate your wounds
I hard His voice just above a whisper
But clear and he said "Hold me so I can find some relief"
I put my arms around Him When He asked "What do you want?"
I said "To know the agony of your passion."

No sooner did I say that when I was filled
With pain from head to toe and began shaking severely
My knees buckled and I knew that I was going to die
I shook severely and I felt the blood from His side would was across my face
But I did nothing to stop it, but continued holding onto Him
The shaking eased somewhat and I knew I was going to live

Suddenly, there was a bright light in front of me
And as I opened my eyes, I knew the agony of His passion was mine
I looked into the light and saw what looked a like a host
I received his body, blood, soul and divinity in that moment
After which, I fell to the floor
Rising I told Him I would come back the next day and share the agony
Of his passion in a better way. The crucifix became very quiet and frozen
I left the church knowing I would be back and do better in sharing
His passion. I knew I would do better in His love
My Life was His from now on and as I walked slowly out of the church
His pain was with me.

Prayer Book Page 225

Wed, 13 Feb 2019 13:02:01

Eternal God, Jesus, Love, My Love,
Holy One, there is much sorrow in being separated
from you through an active choice to
be away from you in darkness.
Loneliness fills the hour away from you
settling in the darkness
There are many expressions of suffering
in separation from you.
We fulfill life's requirements in
Finding a special way to embrace
you to share the agony of your great suffering
and passion on the cross. All done
for us, the perpetrators of your cross

It's time to realize the ambitions of the soul
Let the light of the soul enter all things and make
them holy. love lives where
the light of the soul illuminates
It is easy to live in the light of salvation
Desire has to lead a person with his own soul to God

Prayer Book Page 227

Thu, 28 Feb 2019 14:02:36

Eternal God, Jesus, Love
My Love, Time is locked
into redemption from the moment of your
Crucifixion and death on the cross, to the present time,
It will hold true until the end of time.
The mystery of redemption
Will go on until the last soul
Is called into the kingdom

Because of the working of the Holy Spirit
Which remains a mystery, Almighty God is close
To humanity.
To understand the mystery of redemption
It is necessary to understand the Holy Spirit

Pray that you can enter the mystery
Of Redemption To live and die in the
Agony and passion of the crucifixion
of the Son of God - Jesus Christ

Prayer Book Page 228

Tue, 05 Mar 2019 16:01:36

Eternal God, Jesus, Love,
My Love, As life is lived
We find ourselves longing
For the embrace of the divine
Love and Glory

The marvelous way of divine love
takes away the shadows and our
Souls are filled with divine light

This day continues in the warmth
of your love, Holy One, and in anticipation
Of what is waiting for us.

We live in your mercy and pray to live in your everlasting love.

Prayer Book Page 229

Tue, 12 Mar 2019 09:37:43

Eternal God, Jesus, Love
My Love, Holy One, it is time
To remember your pain and suffering.
Your suffering on the cross demonstrates a
Silent loyalty to your father and
the kingdom. It is not easy
To pass through what you did and remain forgiving
We know those closer to you
Suffered along with you
Enduring the wounds of sacrifice
To redeem mankind for not being loyal to you
Holy One, We try to se you
Without success we are not
given to holiness or
share in your suffering
on the cross

Prayer Book Page 230

Mon, 18 Mar 2019 10:27:46

Eternal God, Jesus, Love
My Love, Holy One, in your
Light many blessings are received
That fill the soul with peace and love
It can be experienced in a soft and magnetic way
In the purity of the moment
One can experience the grace of you.
It is experienced to such and extent
The soul almost
Surrenders its own life to you.
One can speak and taste the goodness of you
Out of eternal consent
One is freely absorbed into you to live.
The only desire living in the soul is to be
with you.
Peace does not come until the soul is
Free to live in you, Holy One.

Prayer Book Page 231

Thu, 28 Mar 2019 16:02:12

Eternal God, Jesus, Love, It has been brought to, Holy One,
to your attention
the horrible amount of sick people here before us.
We are trying to pray for your love
to embrace and help them to get better
Many of them may not recover without your healing love.
It is not continuous
it is not only the prayers offered to them to get better
But for your healing love to embrace them.

We reach in devout love to your embracing healing
love remembering your days in the past
Grant peace and healing Holy One, and if need be
The Glory of Eternal life

Prayer Book Page 232

Mon, 01 Apr 2019 16:19:34

Eternal God, Jesus, Love, My Love,
reaching for you is very difficult in trying
to be one with you.
As you are one with the Father.

The inclination of reaching for the gift
of grace can at times be very misleading
Doubt becomes all consuming when reaching for the
goodness of you Holy One

Prayer seeks to obtain from you, Holy One, the
gift of your grace to give life tot he soul.
The vision of glory arrives when you, Holy One
visit the soul.

In the collection of hours from agony in the garden
to the time you give up your spirit into the hands of your father, we hold
you to share the terrible suffering.
it is not easy in any way to hold you through these hours.
We nevertheless, must live in
your suffering.
It is only through love that truth is known.

Prayer Book Page 233

Tue, 09 Apr 2019 16:33:27

Eternal God, Jesus Love

My love it is time to bring to your divine attention, the suffering souls who reach for you at their peril.

Some are held in concentration camps or prisons where they are tortured and killed because they search for You. Please give them Your love and fill their heart with peace.

Long term suffering is endured for reaching for You in your divine love. Somehow lift them up with real hope to trust in your love.

Remember all of them Holy One, reach for them as they reach for you. Many are betrayed by their need for money. Every day in prison they wait in the hope that you will give them faith.

There is much to say on their behalf. Join them in their prayers so given to You,
Holy One, in their torture.

Still in their prayers they reach for you. In their life of prayer as prisoners they reach for you. It is a rare gift they will not surrender their love for You. Nothing is temporary. They will die before giving up their love for You.

In the end, it will be found in their suffering there is *Resurrection*.

Prayer Book Page 234

Fri, 17 May 2019 12:42:10

Eternal God, Jesus, Love, My Love,
Holy One, Surely you know that recently over 200 people were
murdered. Please call them
into your Kingdom and fan the fires of hell for the murderers.

Holy One, look with divine compassion upon all the souls
murdered in callous disregard.

They stand in heaven's light waiting for you, Holy One, to embrace them
and grant them eternal life, while the fires of hell brighten, Angels
are weeping for Sri Lanka.

Prayer Book Page 235

Tue, 28 May 2019 09:09:09

Eternal God, Jesus, Love,
My Love, Holy One, There is a serious question that has to be presented to
you for our understanding.

Why?

Why did you suffer such terrible pain in the crucifixion?
The brutality of it causes one to ask why?

How did your Father allow that terrible pain to tear you apart, all the way
from your crown of thorns to your scourging?

It is in disbelief that we hold you in faith while your blood flows.

Maybe someday you will provide an answer as to why you suffered so terribly.

We are able to receive you in the Eucharist, but we are unable to share your
pain and suffering.

Not wanting to be separated from you, in the brutality of your crucifixion,
we do offer our love to be of comfort to you.

Prayer Book Page 236

Thu, 30 May 2019 08:40:52

Eternal God, Jesus, Love
My Love, It is so difficult trying to understand
the great mystery of you in your crucifixion.

The question arises as to why.

What in all of heaven did you see in humanity that would cause
you such a bitter sacrifice.

Any reasonable person would want to understand the extent of your suffering
There is obviously a lack of caring of all those involved, in their brutality in their
hatred of you.

Prayer Book Page 237

Tue, 04 Jun 2019 09:48:50

Eternal God, Jesus, Love,
My Love, it is difficult to live with the though that so many people have abandoned you
and no longer hold within themselves you sacrifice.

We can see in the modern world the total disregard for you and your love.
One can only wonder what has happened that so many have abandoned your Holiness and the magnitude for your sacrifice

Coldness of heart by those who should be grateful compounds the problem for humanity.
Eternal death

Prayer Book Page 238

Fri, 14 Jun 2019 09:14:48

Eternal God, Jesus Love, My Love
It is time to bring your attention to the
great persecution of your people - it is difficult to imagine the
extent of their suffering.
Many of them pray for relief only to end up being slain.
Death brings an end to their suffering.
It is difficult to understand why your people are slain without mercy
Others who follow your word should surely pray for your brothers and sisters
We can only live with hope sharing in their suffering of your people.
Peace comes only in prayer.
Your people are slain reaching for you.
Holy One, grant them your mercy.

Prayer Book Page 239

Tue, 09 Jul 2019 11:53:19

Eternal God, Jesus, Love, Holy One
Grant the grace for us to share in the understanding the agony of your passion.
Include the brutality of every minute.

This prayer is offered, Holy One, to enable us to transcend between us and your cross.
We want to learn about your suffering on the cross.
We seek to comfort you by not only witnessing your crucifixion but by living on the cross with you,
We seek redemption you offered in your sacrifice.

Prayer Book Page 240

Eternal God, Jesus, Love, Holy One,
This prayer is very special and is placed directly into your Sacred Heart.
It is about a young lady who died from bone cancer.
I thought to myself, this young lady, I would have healed if I could, and I ask myself
Why with your glorious power, you did not heal her yourself.
Her name is Kaitlyn Rose Bernhardt, a lovely young lady I couldn't believe that bone cancer destroyed her.
Reaching out beyond the heavens I offer this special prayer that you will call her quickly into your kingdom and
Everlasting love and peace.
It wasn't until I read the entire article that I realized what happened to her.
She is a teenager and there have been calls for her sainthood.
I choose to believe that you have already lifted this young lady high up in your kingdom.
The entire story left me utterly sad and shaken because it does appear once we get sick we pass away quickly
I pray you will bless Kaitlyn and give her rest and life in you.
When my day comes when I join Kaitlyn with the saints, and angels, I will visit in my own resurrection.

Prayer Book Page 241

Mon, 22 Jul 2019 11:59:55

Eternal God, Jesus, Love, Holy One,
For sure, we have to remember to petition you for the grace of divine mercy
So many times, Holy One, we find ourselves in serious situations that can spiral out of control.
All we have left is to reach for you, Holy One, and remember your brutal passion and pray for your help.

Many times we find ourselves in the anxiety filled situations which we cannot handle.
There is only one way to go. We have to reach for you, Holy One, for strength, calmness and peace.
We do this by living in your passion. We know that in your passion we can find peace and comfort.
We cannot suffer the lose of you. We live in your eternal love, and reach for you to embrace you in unifying prayer to
experience you glory eternal God.

Prayer Book Page 242

Mon, 22 Jul 2019 12:03:17

Eternal God, Jesus, Love, Holy One, we have to bring to your attention the suffering of so many.
It is difficult to keep calm after sitting in quiet prayer for an hour and no know if goodness was coming.
It is difficult to accept only silence.
The prayer is very sincere and seeks only goodness.
Divine love is the answer that you give freely, Holy One, from the depth of your sacred passion.

Prayer Book Page 243

Wed, 21 Aug 2019 15:59:15

Eternal God, Jesus, Love, Holy One,
I know you are aware there is a rose in heaven which has blossomed out of suffering.
Shower graces on Rose, lifting her up to be with the saints.
Let it be seen through Rose's pain and suffering mysteriously brings life.
This is exactly what happened to Kaitlyn Rose, who will live eternally in God's divine love
Kaitlyn Rose is now among the blessed.

Prayer Book Page 244

Wed, 21 Aug 2019 16:02:44

Eternal God, Jesus, My Love, Holy One,
it is important to bring to your attention the lack of communication after praying.
There has to be a way we can tell that our prayers have reached you when all there is,
is silence, after at least an hour of praying. Looking into our eyes tells me you are there, but only in silence.
Your silence is unbearable when death arrives. We weep in the silence with no hope of communication.
In the focus of a moment reality becomes clear.

Prayer Book Page 245

Wed, 28 Aug 2019 13:17:55

Eternal God, Jesus, Love, Holy One,
sitting in silence, praying with your picture at my right hand, I noticed the right eye is looking straight at me with the left eye off to the side looking somewhere else. The right eye is immovable but very clear. I really can't tell where the left eye is looking. Slowly the left eye moves to join the right eye. Now both eyes are looking together, straight at me.

The face is open and almost clear, to a point where it appears that a smile will burst forward any second. The eyes are very revealing reaching a point of being alive. With both eyes alive life is shared between two people. One person received more life giving grace than the other. Every view is spiritual manifestation. From the eyes is given life. Divine life

Prayer Book Page 246

Mon, 09 Sep 2019 14:19:21

Eternal God, Jesus, Love,
Holy One, must bring to you r attention how many people live in the deep
pit of hate.
One must think what they do when a need arises and they must turn to you
with the ugliness of ate in their hearts

When their need is to serious they have to shift their lives to think what to do.
When they stand in front of you, how will they explain their souls filled with
hatred?
Hell is filled with souls who have lived in hate.
The future for them is very bleak.
Love is the only path to heaven
Everybody is free to choose what path they will take

Mixed crowds travel the same road.
Love is mixed with hate.
The expectancy is love will reign supreme.
It must be remembered by all that God is a witness of how each individual
feels.
The goat will go to the left.
The rest will join the lamb in joy and peace

Heaven will live for those who seek it and their freedom is in their love.
Love is the secret of life.

Prayer Book Page 247

Eternal God, Jesus, Love, Holy One, Looking into your eyes, your face seems to glow and I know you are there, but it seems that our eternal Father does not allow us to cross the line to hear your voice. It is difficult to understand why this is o. You appeared at Fatima, Lourdes and many other places. I don't understand why we can't hear your voice, especially since we know you suffered in the brutal Passion of your Son. We should have the opportunity to thank you for being faithful during the brutality of that Passion. How wonderful it would be for you to speak, please pray the Father, would allow us to communicate. The only person that had a wonderful chance was St. John, when he took your arm to support you at the direction of your Son, Jesus. This prayer is offered as the only prayer to heaven.

Prayer Book Page 248

Eternal God, Jesus, Love, Holy One, Splattered with blood, the stone cried out. There were two sounds. One, the moaning and groaning of Christians being torn apart by savage lions, the other, cheering mobs rejoicing at the slaughter.

Heaven was silent.

Now, in our modern time, the slaughter the abuses continue on a much exaggerated level. The killing is now completed with all kinds of weapons. Many Christians are killed or sent to concentration camps. The weapons assured that the killing is complete in large numbers. One can see the violations of life and freedom throughout the world. Many of the dead are martyrs in the sense of the word. Many will go to hell after their last breath. WE pray God gathers in his children giving them eternal life.

Prayer Book Page 249

Thu, 26 Sep 2019 11:40:38

Eternal God, Jesus, Love, Holy One, it is absolutely necessary to view the day of your Mother. I have concluded, after looking into her eyes for many days, finding the truth.

MOTHER

Mother of God
Mother of Hope
Mother of the Resurrection
Mother of the Eucharist
Mother of Redemption
Mother of the Ascension
Mother of Forgiveness
Mother of the Passion
Mother of Humility

Your Mother is also my Mother. All these things and more, she became the when she told the angel, "Be it done unto me according to your word."

Everyday I search your eyes trying to find you, Mother.

Prayer Book Page 250

Fri, 04 Oct 2019 14:56:53

Eternal God, Jesus, Love,

Holy One,

Long ago it happened, the Angel stood in front of a young lady
and had a conversation with her.

It ends with the words *"Be it done unto me according to thy Word."*

The greatest mystery is that all of history began. The ultimate sacrifice would
be concluded. The sacrificial lamb would experience the most brutal passion
and die.
One cannot conceive of such an event that the Son of God would suffer and
die. The salvation of mankind would be secured.

It was the beginning but there is no end to the Mystery of the Passion. Our
God is eternal and will not allow the violent and brutal Passion of His only
Son to slip away and be forgotten. It will be hell if mankind forgets. There will
be no Resurrection for those who through faith know Jesus as the sacrificial
Lamb but turn against Him for worldly pleasures.

Prayer Book Page 251

Posted on November 3, 2019 by dirtinyoureye

Eternal God, Jesus, Love

Holy One, an ungodly stench rises out of the "House" where secret meetings have been
taking place, designed to suffocate the people and destroy the country. Born in darkness, they can only produce rotten fruit. The evil will lead to people in war against people in violent flashes. There will be civil war, marshal law, with many people dying. This will all take place in the absence of divinity with man in complete destruction.

Hate prevails.

Those who live and die in hate will not wake up to Resurrection but to eternal darkness. They will never see the light of true life...

Printed in the United States
By Bookmasters